VICTORIA'S NAVY

of the sailing navy

KENNETH MASON

TO MOTHER AND FATHER

ISBN 085937 2243

© **Colin White 1981**

All rights reserved. No part of this publication
may be reproduced, stored in a retrieval system or
transmitted, in any form or by any means, electronic,
mechanical, photocopying, recording or otherwise,
without the prior permission of the copyright owner.

British Library Cataloguing in Publication Data
White, Colin
The end of the sailing navy.
1. Great Britain. Royal Navy — History
    — 19th century
1. Title
359'.00941 VA454

ISBN 0-85937-224-3

Published by Kenneth Mason, Homewell, Havant, Hampshire

Produced in Great Britain by Articulate Studios, Emsworth
Designed by Sadlergraphics

4

ACKNOWLEDGEMENTS

All the prints, paintings and photographs used in this book have
been taken from the collections of the Royal Naval Museum,
Portsmouth.
The woodcuts and line-engravings come from the *Illustrated
London News* (Vols 1 - 56).
The photograph of the ceramic figure of Thomas Cooke on page
82 is reproduced by kind permission of Antony Oliver, Esq.
The medals on pages 73, 81 and 88 and the engraving of the *Royal
Sovereign* on page 92 come from the collection of Captain K J
Douglas-Morris, DL, RN and are reproduced with his kind
permission.

The end of the sailing navy

THE GRAND NAVAL REVIEW.

The end

COLIN WHITE

**FOREWORD BY ADMIRAL OF THE FLEET
SIR TERENCE LEWIN GCB MVO DSC DSc
CHIEF OF THE DEFENCE STAFF**

SIGNAL FOR AN ENGAGEMENT — HOME
One of a pair of engravings by J Fairburn, published
in 1838 (See also page 62)

Contents

As a great admirer and supporter of the Royal Naval Museum, Portsmouth, I am delighted to have been asked to write the foreword for this book. It gives me an opportunity to congratulate Colin White, who here chronicles a little known period in the history of the Royal Navy; and the Museum, because publication coincides with the opening of a major and exciting new exhibition — 'The end of the sailing navy'. Most of the fascinating illustrations in the book are from the Museum's growing collection. ¶ The reign of Queen Victoria saw the consolidation of a British Empire founded on the strength and ubiquity of sea power. The Royal Navy had emerged all powerful from the Napoleonic Wars and it would have been all too easy to rest on the laurels won at great victories, St Vincent, Nile, Trafalgar. It was the era of Pax Britannica. Yet in this period the Royal Navy not only grappled with a rate of technological change greater than any during the previous five hundred years but was engaged in action and exploration on sea and land on a wider scale than ever

before. ¶ In this splendidly comprehensive book Colin White describes vividly the

Foreword

traumas that accompanied the end of sail and the introduction of steam against the background of the Victorian age. While the effect on ships and equipment is clear to see, there had to be as great a change in the mental attitude of those brought up in the age of sail. It is particularly interesting to read that, perhaps because of preoccupation with material innovation, conditions of service on board changed little. It remained a hard life on the lower deck. ❡ *In our own time the Royal Navy has been facing up to as great a change as our Victorian predecessors: nuclear propulsion, and the true submarine, long range precision missiles, nuclear weapons, air power, the great social revolution of the twentieth century. Colin White helps us to look back and check that we have learnt the lessons of history.*

ADMIRAL OF THE FLEET SIR TERENCE LEWIN GCB MVO DSC DSc

Chief of the Defence Staff

In 1815, Britain finally emerged from the greatest of all her wars with France. It had lasted for twenty-two years with only a short break; had involved more than ten major nations and had been waged in all corners of the globe — from the East Indies to the western seaboard of South America and from the Shetlands to South Africa. A whole generation had grown up in the shadow of war and the map of the world — especially in Europe — had been drastically changed. To the Victorians, it was simply *The Great War* — and this description will be used in the ensuing pages to avoid monotonous repetition of its more correct modern title '*The French Revolutionary and Napoleonic Wars*'!

Although such a monumental conflict had called for an immense effort on the part of Britain — the only country that remained fighting against the French for the entire war — it had nonetheless established her in a unique position as the dominant world power. In part, this position was due to her victories for, although the war was decided on the battlefields of Europe, Britain's main efforts had been directed at the overseas colonies of her enemies and her sea power had won for her a number of important possessions which gave her footholds in most of the important strategic areas of the world. But even more important was her great economic strength. Her overseas trade had not only survived the acute strains of the war but had in fact emerged considerably strengthened, while the commerce of her main rivals — France, Spain and Holland — had been crushed. Moreover, the war had considerably accelerated Britain's industrial revolution, which meant that she was years ahead of her neighbours — literally the 'workshop of the world'. As a result, in the great period of expansion and change which followed Waterloo, Britain had a head start; indeed, she led the field until well into the second half of the century.

The great bulwark of Britain's supremacy was her Navy — and here, too, dramatic changes were taking place. Over the years, the Victorian Navy has acquired a reputation for unthinking conservatism and the stories are rife of reactionary admirals who preferred the beauty and cleanliness of sail to the steam engine, with all its attendant dirt, and who thought that spotless paintwork and gleaming brasswork were more important indicators of a ship's efficiency than the standard of her gunnery. Such admirals existed of course, but, as always, the stories have been exaggerated and this book's main aim is to try to redress the balance a little. During the reign of Queen Victoria, the Navy, in common with the rest of society, underwent a technological and social revolution that has been equalled only by the great upheavals of our own day. The magnificent, towering ships of the line (or *battleships,* as they will be called throughout this book) were altered and adapted until finally they were replaced altogether by the ugly, squat, black-hulled ironclads. The rough, part-time seamen gave way to literate, full-time, professional sailors. Living conditions, training, pay, pensions, and uniforms: all aspects of life afloat passed under review. And all these changes had to be undertaken in a period when the growing demands of the ever-expanding Empire meant that the Navy was busier, more widely engaged and more over-stretched than ever before in peacetime.

Because of the complexity of the story and the wealth of material

The end of the sailing navy

available, the period has been divided into two and each section dealt with in separate books. Although called *Victoria's Navy*, the series in fact begins in 1830— the year of the accession of William IV — because a number of important social and technological developments, which are vital to the story, took place in the decade 1830-40. Similarly, the second book will end not with Victoria's death but with the death of her son, Edward VII, in 1910 so that the final eclipse of the Victorian fleet by the *Dreadnought* and her successors can be dealt with. Dates and titles are, after all, very arbitrary divisions but it is hoped that, within these very broad limits, some coherent structure will be discerned!

The illustrations other than *Illustrated London News* engravings, have been taken from the collections of the Royal Naval Museum. This is conscious policy. For the last five years, the museum has deliberately concentrated both its research and its collecting resources very heavily on the Victorian period, with the result that it now possesses one of the best Victorian naval collections in the country. A part of that collection will be placed on permanent display in two major new exhibitions during the next few years but by no means all the paintings, prints and photographs can be shown at one time — hence this book.

I am very grateful for the help and encouragement which I have received from all my colleagues — but my thanks are due especially to the Museum Director, Ray Parsons, whose constant support has been decisive. And, while I am dealing with the museum, it would be appropriate to record here my gratitude to one of our foremost benefactors, Kenneth Douglas-Morris. All the *Illustrated London News* engravings come from his splendid collection, now in the museum's library, and I have unashamedly drawn on his unique knowledge of the social and numismatic history of the Victorian Navy in preparing my third chapter. I am also grateful for the great interest shown in this project by Sir Terence Lewin, the Chief of the Defence Staff and a notable friend of the museum, who has most kindly contributed the Foreword.

Every book is the result of teamwork and never more so than when the author is young and inexperienced. My mother, Margaret White, deciphered my manuscript and typed it out, while my father, Philip White, read and corrected the final text. I have also relied heavily — and thankfully! — on the wisdom and expertise of my publisher Kenneth Mason and his colleague Bob Anderson without whose friendly advice my small store of confidence would have vanished long ago. And, because this is first and foremost an illustrated book, it owes even more than usual to its designer, Geoff Sadler, who has managed to turn the unco-ordinated batch of text and illustrations with which I confronted him into a logical and attractive sequence. To all, my grateful thanks, for this is as much their book as mine— although, naturally, the ultimate responsibility for any mistakes or omissions lies squarely on my shoulders!

Colin S White
June 1980 Alverstoke, Hampshire 9

The Experimental Brigs circa 1850
In the foreground is HMS Flying Fish, launched in 1844 and designed by Sir William Symonds

THE NAVY IN 1830 was still very much as Nelson had known it. Of the 14 battleships in active service one, HMS *Revenge*, had fought at Trafalgar and three others had been in the fleet during his lifetime. There were 80 other battleships building or 'in ordinary' (reserve) and eleven of these had fought at Trafalgar, including, of course, HMS *Victory*, which was still in commission as the Port Admiral's flagship at Portsmouth. Indeed, in 1830 a rumour began circulating that she was to be heavily rebuilt or even broken up, but public feeling was so strong that the old ship was saved. As for the personnel of the fleet, the list of admirals in active employment read like a roll-call of Nelson's captains. Sir Henry Blackwood was in command at the Nore; Sir James Saumarez at Plymouth; and Sir Thomas Foley at Portsmouth. Sir Richard Keats was Governor of Greenwich Hospital and under him, as Chief Physician, was Dr William Beatty, the man who had nursed Nelson on his death-bed. And the professional head of the service, the First Sea Lord, was none other than Sir Thomas Masterman Hardy.

Nonetheless, there had been a number of important technological changes in the fleet since 1805. Anchor cables were made of iron chain instead of hemp. Many of the ships' internal fittings — including parts of their actual framework — were made of iron. The 'waist', the open space in the middle of the upper deck between the quarterdeck and the fo'c'sle, had been closed in, giving a clean sweep from bow to stern. And the ships were more solidly constructed. Nelsonian warships had showed a tendency to 'hog' — in other words, to arch upwards in the middle — because the support from the water was relatively greater

amidships than at the bow and stern. This caused serious stresses, especially when the ship was in heavy weather. Captain Brenton, who served in the Great War, recalled: ' . . . I remember well, when I was a midshipman in a 64-gun ship coming home from India, cracking nuts by the working of the ship. We put them in under the knees, as she rolled one way and snatched them out as she rolled back again . . . ' Sir Robert Seppings, who was Surveyor of the Navy between 1813 and 1832, countered this problem by introducing diagonal bracing between the standard rectangular frames of the ships. As a result, ships were not only stronger and stiffer but also they could be made much longer than before. The *Victory's* lower gundeck was 186 feet long and she carried 104 guns on three decks. HMS *Victoria*, which was launched in 1853, also had three gundecks but she mounted 131 guns and her lower gundeck was 250 feet long.

Another important limitation of ships such as the *Victory* had been the weakness of their bows and sterns, which made them very vulnerable to end-on 'raking' fire. Seppings did away with the old flat sterns with their light construction and colourful but useless decoration and replaced them with round, solidly built structures which were pierced by numerous gunports. Similarly, bows were made bluffer and were framed in right up to the bowsprit. None of these ships could have been knocked out by a single raking broadside through the stern, as happened to the unfortunate French flagship *Bucentaure* at Trafalgar.

These improvements to the sailing fleet were continued by Captain William Symonds RN, who became Surveyor in 1832 and

11

continued in office until 1847. He caused much controversy with his new ideas on ship construction but undoubtedly he deserves the credit for having designed some of the fastest sailing warships of all classes that ever served in the Royal Navy. Most important of all, he introduced the concept of standardised fittings — especially for masts, yards and rigging — which greatly simplified the problem of providing 'spare parts'.

However, the most significant difference between the fleet of 1830 and that of 1805, lay not in the great battleships but at the opposite end of the list of ships in commission. For there, among the smallest vessels were eight little steamers. Only two of them actually carried guns, but their presence in the Navy List alongside the sailing warships indicated that the changes were already under way which were completely to revolutionise the Navy by 1870.

Although steam engines were in common use on land, especially in Britain, long before the outbreak of the Great War, it was not until 1801 that the first successful river steamboat was built — the *Charlotte Dundas*. Seagoing vessels took longer to develop but, in 1821, a steam packet service was introduced to carry the mails between Holyhead and Dublin and, in the same year, a steamer called the *Monkey* was purchased by the Admiralty for use as a tug. The following year, the *Comet* was brought into service and to her goes the distinction of being the first steam vessel actually ordered and built expressly for the Navy. Thereafter, the number of tugs and packet boats grew rapidly and, although only eight steamers were actually mentioned in the 1830 Navy List, there were many other humbler steam craft in service by this time. The

HMS Eurydice c 1850

This 26-gun frigate was launched in 1843. She became a boys' training ship in 1861 and was lost with nearly all hands off the Isle of Wight in 1878

Improvements in the sailing fleet

Under two successive Surveyors of the Navy, Sir Robert Seppings (1813-1832) and Sir William Symonds (1832-1847), the design of British warships was gradually improved. Ships became longer, more sturdy and better sailers

growing importance of steam propulsion was acknowledged by the creation in 1833 of a special 'Steam Factory' at Woolwich Dockyard where engineers could be trained and new machinery tested. And in 1837 a special branch of naval engineers was formed. Hitherto, the machinery had been manned by men who had been sent aboard by the company which fitted the engines and, as 'mere labourers', they had been accorded only lower deck status. Now, for the first time, their officers were appointed by warrant and so became an integral part of the naval hierarchy.

Despite these important advances, steam propulsion remained limited throughout the 1830s to small warships and auxiliaries; while the frigates and battleships continued to be built with sails only. This was not unthinking conservatism. In the first place, paddlewheels, which were at this time the only form of propulsion available, were most unsuitable for warships. They offered large and vulnerable targets to enemy shot. They took up space which would otherwise have been occupied by broadside guns, thus considerably reducing a ship's firepower. And the machinery required to drive them filled the entire midships section and protruded well above the waterline — providing another excellent target. It is scarcely surprising that battleship designers continued to rely on sails.

These technical limitations were reinforced by official policy for, throughout the Victorian period, the Admiralty consistently refused to introduce any striking innovations, until forced to by a foreign power. There were sound reasons for such a policy. First,

The Stern of HMS Asia

A 74-gun battleship, launched in Bombay in 1824. She was Codrington's flagship at Navarino 1827 and had a distinctive, rounded Seppings stern pierced for numerous gunports

Breaking up of HMS Ganges 1929

Launched in Bombay in 1821 she ended her career as a boys' training ship at Shotley, Suffolk. In this photograph her Seppings diagonal bracing which gave her hull additional strength is clearly visible

The Paddle Frigates

Steam engines were fitted in small warships in the early 1830s but the large paddle wheels and their machinery took up a large amount of valuable space and were vulnerable to enemy fire. Thus it was some time before they were fitted to larger ships such as heavy frigates

HMS Penelope 1843

Laid down 1829 she was launched as a paddle frigate in 1842. Pennant ship of Commodore, West Africa Squadron 1843, HMS Penelope was the first steamer to serve as a permanent flagship.

Britain already possessed command of the seas and it would have been foolish to undermine that command by adopting new inventions needlessly. Secondly, this was a period of rapid technological change and many of the new developments were highly experimental. Better therefore to rely upon tried and trusted material until the new methods had fully proved themselves. Above all, the Admiralty could confidently place its trust in the knowledge that Britain was at that time the most advanced industrial nation in the world and so was able, if compelled, easily to outbuild any of her rivals. These were the thoughts which lay behind the famous minute written by Lord Melville, the First Lord of the Admiralty, in 1828 — a statement which has so often before been quoted as a supreme example of official Victorian conservatism:

' . . . Their Lordships . . . feel it their bounden duty to discourage to the utmost of their ability the employment of steam vessels, as they consider that the introduction of steam is calculated to strike a fatal blow at the Naval Supremacy of the Empire . . . '

In fact, as it turned out, the Admiralty had very little opportunity for conservatism. France had learned the importance of seapower during the Great War but she had also learned that she could not hope to break Britain's supremacy at sea by traditional means. Throughout the nineteenth century, her naval thinkers searched for novel ideas by means of which the Royal Navy's battlefleets could be eliminated by small, manoeuvrable and relatively inexpensive vessels, mounting the most up-to-date weapons. And for such a purpose, steam vessels were of course ideal. In 1844, a high

HMS Gladiator 1855

Launched in 1844, HMS Gladiator's design was an attempt to make good the loss of firepower caused by paddle wheel machinery by mounting powerful guns on pivots on the upper deck. She had two 110 pounders mounted in this way and four lighter guns

HMS Leopard c 1865

Her huge hull — 218 by 37½ feet — enabled her to carry five 110 pounders on her upper deck as well as twelve lighter guns on her gun deck. She was launched in 1850

Sectional view of a Paddle Frigate

Note how much room is taken up by the boilers and machinery, thus reducing the number of guns. Note also how they protrude well above the waterline, where they are particularly vulnerable

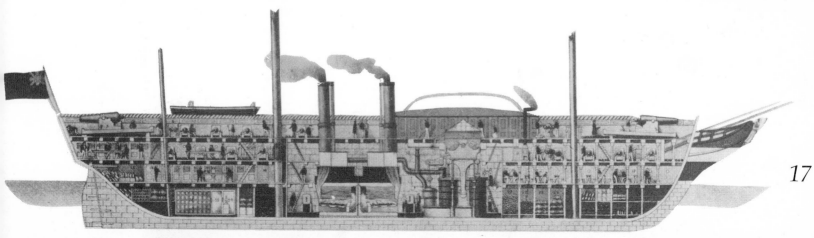

17

HMS Terrible 1856
One of the largest paddle frigates ever built, 226 by 42½ feet,
carrying eight 68 pounders and eleven lighter guns.
She played a prominent part in the Black Sea campaign
of the Crimean War

The coming of screw propulsion

After a series of exhaustive tests, the Admiralty finally decided in the early 1840s to fit screw propellers to its warships. Since screw engines were far more compact than paddle wheel engines, this meant that steam propulsion could at last be fitted to larger ships — including battleships

The Launch of HMS Rattler
The first screw warship, HMS Rattler took part in a series of trials in 1845 with the paddlesloop HMS Alecto, which finally established the ascendancy of the screw propeller

ranking French admiral, the Prince de Joinville, wrote an article pointing out that steamships had not only rendered Britain's sailing navy obsolete, but also that they had made possible a lightning invasion across the Channel. This article was followed by a great and costly French building plan in which steamships featured largely.

In Britain, the French preoccupation with steamships caused an invasion scare in 1844-6, the first of a number of scares which occurred at regular intervals throughout the century. Even the ageing Duke of Wellington expressed the opinion that there was no place on the south coast between Dover and Portsmouth where infantry could not land at any state of the tide or weather. There was a sudden upsurge of interest in coastal defence — fortresses, garrisons and even local volunteer militia — and the Admiralty decided that the time had come to build some large steam frigates. In 1842, a sailing frigate, HMS *Penelope* had been cut in half and lengthened by about 65 feet to enable engines of 650 hp to be fitted. These had given her a top speed of about 10 knots but the weight of her broadside had been considerably reduced, since she was able to mount only 16 guns instead of the 46 for which she had been originally designed. In the new frigates of 1844-6, this weakness was partly countered by equipping the ships with small numbers of very heavy guns and by mounting them on pivots on the upper deck instead of in the traditional broadside position. HMS *Gladiator*, launched at Woolwich in 1844, had only six guns, but two of them were massive 110 pounders. HMS *Odin*, an even bigger frigate, launched at Deptford in 1846, mounted eighteen

19

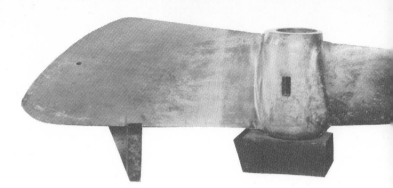

HMS Rattler's propeller

Designed by Sir Francis Pettit Smith, this screw was one of the many experimental designs fitted to her but it proved the most successful. It can still be seen at the Royal Naval Museum, Portsmouth

Screw frigate c 1860

This water colour by W. E. Atkins shows a mid-Victorian sail and steam frigate entering Portsmouth Harbour

HMS Rattler and Alecto 1845
The two ships carried out many tests together but the most dramatic was the tug-of-war shown here. The Rattler succeeded in towing the Alecto sternforemost at more than five knots

HMS Topaze off the Naval Hospital in Bighi Bay, Malta c 1865

A typical example of the huge screw frigates built in the last days of wooden warships. She measured 235 feet by 50 feet and carried 51 guns. She was launched in 1858

22

23

The launch of HMS Amphion
The first screw frigate was launched on January 14, 1846 and converted to steam while still on the stocks. Although 50 feet shorter than the large paddle frigates, her compact screw engines meant that she could carry a full complement of 30 guns mounted in the traditional broadside fashion

HMS Queen c 1865

Launched as a sailing battleship in 1839 HMS Queen took part in the Crimean War, especially the bombardment of Sebastopol, where she was set on fire several times. Converted to steam in 1859

guns of which twelve were mounted broadside, with the remaining six — all of them heavy — on the upper deck. Perhaps the greatest paddle frigate of all was HMS *Terrible*, launched at Deptford in 1846. Like her sisters, she carried heavy pivot guns on her upper deck but her firepower was further increased by the great size of her hull. She was 226 feet long with a beam of 42½ feet, and a tonnage of 1,858 builders measurement and, as a result, she was able to carry eight 68 pounders, eight 56 pounders and three 12 pounders — one of the heaviest armaments ever placed in a frigate. Indeed the steam 'frigates' of the late 1840s were a far cry from the frigates of Nelson's fleet. The *Terrible* was almost twice the size of HMS *Euryalus*, the famous ship commanded by Blackwood at Trafalgar, and she fired a broadside of about the same weight as a 74-gun battleship of the Great War fleet.

Nonetheless, although the problem of lack of firepower appeared to have been overcome, these frigates were still very vulnerable because of their paddlewheels and so, even now, no attempt was made to fit steam propulsion to battleships. Then, just at the moment when the paddle frigates were reaching their peak in ships like the *Terrible*, they were overtaken by another development which made them all obsolete but which also established steampower finally in the Navy as the main propulsive force for virtually every class of ship. That development was, of course, the introduction of the screw propeller.

Once again, there were many different experimental screws and, although prototype screw ships had been built in the mid-1830s, it was not until the mid-1840s that the new form of propulsion finally

HMS Revenge c 1865

A screw battleship of 91 guns, launched in 1859. She was soon overtaken by the new ironclads and relegated to the Coastguard service after only two active commissions. Her funnel is just visible between the main and fore masts

Launch of HMS Windsor Castle

Renamed Duke of Wellington a few days after the launch on September 14, 1852 she became one of the most famous of all the wooden steam battleships (see page 26)

HMS Conqueror 1867

Launched as a sailing battleship, HMS Waterloo in 1833, she was converted to steam in 1859. Renamed Conqueror in 1862 she took part in the Japanese War in 1864 — the last wooden battleship to fire her guns in anger

HMS Agamemnon 1855

Screw battleship of 91 guns, launched in 1852 — the first battleship designed for steam propulsion. She served with distinction in the Black Sea campaigns of the Crimean War

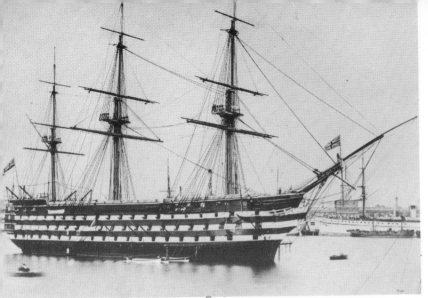

HMS Royal Adelaide c 1870

Launched as a sailing battleship in 1828, she was converted to depot ship in 1860. Served as the flagship of the C-in-C, Plymouth before being broken up in 1905

HMS Duke of Wellington c 1890

Screw battleship of 131 guns and the flagship of the Baltic fleet throughout the Crimean War. Converted for harbour service in 1862 and was the flagship of the C-in-C, Portsmouth for many years before being broken up in 1904

Cut-away view of a screw battleship

Compare with the cut-away of paddle frigate on page 17. Note how the screw machinery is compact enough to be positioned entirely below the waterline where it is well protected and does not interfere with the layout of the guns

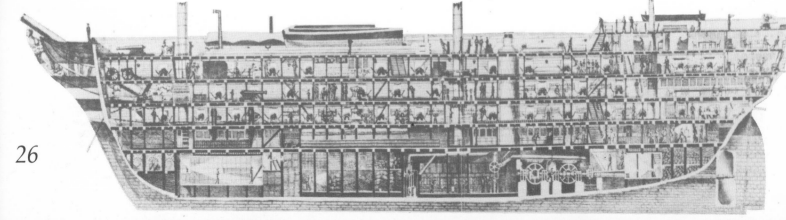

The coming of iron ships

Although iron was used in shipbuilding in the early 1830s, experiments showed that iron hulls had very little resistance to shot and shell. So it was not until the development of strong armour-plating in the late 1850s that iron was first used in the construction of capital ships

established itself. During the winter of 1843-4, the Admiralty fitted a number of different types of screw propeller to a small sloop HMS *Rattler* and tested her performance with them before settling finally on a two-bladed model designed by Sir Francis Pettit Smith. Then, in 1845, a series of trials were held between the *Rattler* and a similarly sized paddlesloop HMS *Alecto* which showed the screw to have decided advantages over the paddle. However, the supporters of paddle-wheels still claimed that they had more pulling power than screws and so the two ships were tied stern to stern and steamed ahead at full power. Slowly but surely the *Rattler* pulled her opponent away at a steady pace. It was the only most dramatic incident in a long series of exhaustive tests, but it nevertheless established the ascendancy of the screw and so finally opened the way for steam propulsion for the entire fleet.

Thereafter, progress became rapid. The building of paddle frigates was eased and, instead, screw frigates were built. The first to be launched in 1846, was a converted sailing frigate, HMS *Amphion* and she was followed by a number of powerful ships designed specifically for screws, some of them mounting as many as 50 guns. But, most significant of all, it now became possible to fit steam propulsion to battleships — especially since the development of horizontal direct-acting engines, which were much more compact than the side-lever paddle engines, meant that a ship's machinery could now be placed completely below the waterline out of harm's way. In 1848, an old 60-gun sailing battleship, HMS *Ajax*, came into service after having been fitted with engines of this type which gave her a top speed of 7 knots.

HMS Birkenhead 1846

Launched in 1845 as an iron paddle frigate and converted to a store and troopship following the adverse results of experiments at HMS Excellent

La Gloire

Following the success of their armoured batteries at Kinburn (see overleaf) the French experimented with full-sized ironclad ships — wooden ships cased in armour-plating. The first of the class was La Gloire and her appearance precipitated the great naval technological revolution of the 1860s

The wreck of HMS Birkenhead
The Birkenhead was tragically lost in Algoa Bay, South Africa, on February 27, 1852 while transporting troops to take part in the third Kaffir War. There was great loss of life, but the occasion was marked by the bravery of the troops who remained lined up on deck as the ship went down, allowing the women and children to escape first

The bombardment of Kinburn

The battle at which armour-plate first proved itself when three new French armoured batteries went into action and survived heavy, close-range fire virtually unscathed on October 17, 1855

And, in 1852, was launched the first battleship designed and built for steam propulsion, with a name that had strong Nelsonian associations: HMS *Agamemnon*. Conversions and new constructions quickly followed and, by 1855, Britain had 20 steam battleships in service — including the aptly-named *James Watt*. All the same, none of these vessels was really a *steamship* in the strictest sense of the word. Their screws were designed simply to give auxiliary power, rather like the small inboard or outboard engines of a modern racing yacht. Indeed, the screws were usually mounted in such a way as to enable them to be hoisted into the body of the ship when she was under sail, so that they would not drag and reduce the speed. Funnels were made telescopic to enable them to be folded out of the way and so, when a ship was preparing to get up steam, the order would be 'Up funnel, down screw!' In fact British designers soon found that it was very difficult to produce a hull shape that suited both sail and steam propulsion equally well. And yet sails were still needed by the Royal Navy at this time. Steam engines were very inefficient and used up large quantities of coal; while British vessels had to be capable of undertaking long voyages to parts of the world where coal was not readily available.

The French designers, unhampered by such global considerations, did rather better. Having watched the British experiments, they decided that performance under sail had to be sacrificed to the needs of screw propulsion. The British decision to abandon the sailing battlefleet gave the French a chance to catch up on their rivals at last and they seized it eagerly. As the 1850s progressed,

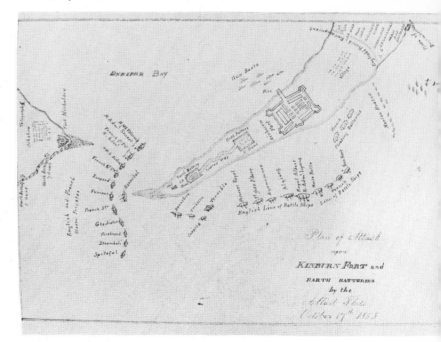

Plan of the bombardment of Kinburn

A page from the personal log-book of Lieutenant Corbett of HMS Gladiator. The three French batteries can be seen on the right of the Franco-British line, close inshore near the fort

HMS WARRIOR 1860

The most revolutionary warship ever built. The challenge posed by the Gloire was met by building a long, iron hull, capable of carrying 36 heavy guns, tough armour plate and engines with a top speed of 14 knots. Thus the Warrior could both out-steam and out-gun all contemporary battleships. She survives today and is being restored by the Maritime Trust prior to going on display at Portsmouth

HMS Glatton 1855

A 14-gun armoured battery of similar design to the French batteries which proved so successful at Kinburn. The first armoured warship in the Royal Navy

they launched increasing numbers of fine wooden battleships all designed primarily as steamships with auxiliary sail power and, by 1858, they had managed for the first time since the seventeenth century to equal the British in numbers of front-line capital ships — 29 steam battleships each. It looked as if the scene was set for a ship-building race which Britain had very little chance of winning outright, since her wooden ship-building capacities were not significantly greater than those of France. But then, at the crucial moment, the eagerness of the French proved their own undoing. In a brave attempt to break Britain's supremacy at a single stroke, they launched a ship that was intended to render all other warships obsolete — the famous armoured frigate, *Gloire*. And she heralded the beginning of a new phase in the development of warship design.

The story of iron warships is inextricably linked with that of naval gunnery and each continued to influence the other throughout the Armoured Battleship period. Guns became increasingly powerful and so more efficient methods of protection had to be devised. This led in turn to the introduction of even bigger guns with greater penetrative power — and so on, in a never-ending game of technological leapfrog. By 1941, it was possible for HMS *Hood*, a powerful battlecruiser with heavy armour-plating, to be destroyed by a single well-aimed shell, but at Trafalgar, in 1805, not a single ship was sunk during the battle as a result of gunfire. The old wooden walls were capable of withstanding a tremendous amount of punishment from the primitive guns of the period, with their solid round shot and so battles were usually decided not by the

HMS Warrior under construction 1860

At this time, none of the Royal Dockyards had the facilities for building iron ships, so this revolutionary vessel was built in a private yard at Blackwall

The Revolutionary Warship c 1870

This photograph, (left) which was taken before her light poop was added in 1872, shows the Warrior's great length and graceful lines. These gave her high speeds under both sail and steam but made her difficult to manoeuvre

(Below) HMS Warrior was fitted with ten breech-loaders of a design which, together with her 26 standard muzzle-loading 68 pounders gave her an immensely powerful broadside that was more than a match for most contemporary battleships

destruction of ships but rather by the number which surrendered because their crews could not fight any longer. So, it was hard and continuous pounding, not accuracy, which brought victory and one of the main reasons why the British had been so successful during the Great War, was that they had been able almost invariably to fire off more broadsides in a shorter space of time than their opponents.

As with steampower, it was the French who first challenged the old methods: this time, with guns that fired explosive shells. Throughout the Great War, Britain had employed a number of small 'bomb vessels', which fired large hollow round shells — usually at fortifications or at ships in harbour. Although the destructive power of these missiles was enormous compared with the standard roundshot, they were more erratic and had much less penetrative power, so the British tended to regard them as weapons for very specialised tasks only. But in France after the war, an artillery expert called Paixhans experimented with smaller shells fired from ordinary guns instead of mortars. These shells were still very erratic and had only a limited range, but Paixhans planned to solve these problems by mounting his new weapons on some of the new steamers, which would then be able to dart among the lumbering British sailing battleships, destroying them one by one with explosive shells at close range, while avoiding their clumsy broadsides of roundshot. This imaginative scheme was never fully tried. The British were also experimenting with the new weapons but, in accordance with their standard policy, the Admiralty saw no reason to embark upon an expensive conversion

HMS Warrior c 1875
This photograph was taken in Portsmouth harbour where she was under refit and shows her distinctive clipper bow

Engine room of HMS Warrior
Note the crinolined lady on the upper gallery

of their armament until a foreign power forced their hand. Eventually, in 1837, the French announced a general change to shell-firing guns and, in less than two years, the British battlefleet had been similarly rearmed. Some solid shot guns continued to be mounted, since they still had greater range than shell guns, but the French had to accept that the new invention had in no way reduced the supremacy of the Royal Navy.

On the other hand, both France and Britain realised that the coming of explosive shells meant that wooden ships were no longer so immune from gunfire and so attempts were made to find new methods of protection. Iron had been used in the construction of merchant ships for some years and, in 1839, the firm of Lairds built two iron paddle war steamers for the Honourable East India Company. Both these ships, the *Nemesis* and the *Phlegethon*, were extremely successful vessels — they rendered sterling service during the First China War and the *Nemesis* gave further proof of the advantages of an iron hull when she grounded on some rocks off Scilly and was saved by her watertight compartments. The Admiralty decided that iron ship construction had advanced sufficiently for use in warships and accordingly, in 1844, they ordered five iron frigates as part of the building programme introduced to counter the new French steamships. The first of these iron ships, HMS *Birkenhead* was launched in 1845 and came into service a year later.

However, neither the *Birkenhead*, nor any of her fellow iron frigates, were destined to serve as warships. While they were still building, the Admiralty ordered a series of tests to be carried out

34

The first generation of ironclads

HMS Warrior was followed by a series of iron-built ships all with strong armour plate. However, the French were building a whole fleet of successors to the Gloire and so, in an attempt to keep ahead, the British also started fitting armour plate to some of their wooden ships. A fierce naval arms race ensued

HMS Black Prince at the Jubilee Review 1887

Launched in 1861 this ship was sister to the Warrior

HMS Agincourt at the Jubilee Review 1887

One of the three famous five-masted ironclads, she was launched in 1865 and ended her career as a coal hulk and lasted until 1960

HMS Achilles c 1880

The first ironclad to be built in a Royal dockyard —
Chatham — and the only one to step four masts. The
fourth mast was removed in 1865 and this photograph
shows her as she appeared throughout most of her career

HMS Achilles in Chatham Dockyard 1863

A contemporary photograph showing the Achilles
under construction. Note the top-hatted dockyard
officials on the left of the platform

36

HMS Achilles under construction 1863
Two engravings from the Illustrated London News showing the Achilles when her hull was half-finished. In the engraving on the left the figures are deliberately made small to exaggerate the size of the ship

on iron vessels to see how they withstood gunfire. The results were horrifying. Solid round shot penetrated the sides as if they were made of paper, making large, jagged holes which would have been very difficult to plug and, worst of all, sending up showers of lethal metal splinters which were every bit as dangerous and far more numerous than the splinters which had caused so many wounds in the old wooden ships. These experiments continued until 1851 and all the results were so unfavourable to iron hulls that the Admiralty converted its iron 'frigates' to troop transports and abandoned all further thoughts of iron warships. The problem of how to protect ships from shellfire was still unsolved.

That problem was further emphasised by actual war experience. In 1853, a Russian fleet, armed predominantly with shell guns, attacked a Turkish fleet of wooden battleships in Sinope Bay and completely destroyed it. The Turks had been outnumbered in any case but the feature of the battle which attracted the most attention was the fact that their ships had been armed only with solid-shot guns and so the Rusians had escaped almost scot-free. The battle was followed quickly by the Crimean War and, on October 17 1854, the lesson was rubbed home yet again when a combined British and French fleet attacked the massive forts guarding the seaward approaches to Sebastopol. None of the ships could get close enough to the forts to do any extensive damage and they were themselves very badly knocked about by the Russian shells. HMS *Queen,* for example, was set on fire three times. Clearly, some method had to be devised of attacking these forts without exposing

HMS Royal Oak
The first of seven wooden battleships which were converted
to ironclads in order to keep Britain ahead in the
naval arms race. One gun deck was removed and
armourplate fitted to the sides

valuable capital ships to destructive shell fire.

The British immediately began building large flotillas of small shallow-draught gunboats mounting two or three very heavy guns but it was the French who devised the most effective answer. Three 'armoured batteries' were built: 60-foot long, shallow-draught ships with auxiliary steampower, armed with sixteen 56-pounder guns and protected with four-inch iron plates, backed with a thick lining of wood. They joined the combined fleet in the Black Sea in 1855, just in time to take part in the bombardment of Kinburn on October 17, and they were an instant success. They were able to get close enough to the Russian forts to pour in a murderous fire, while the enemy shot simply dented their plates slightly and, in the words of the British Commander-in-Chief, Sir Edmund Lyons, left only 'a few rust-like marks.' His report to the Admiralty continued:

'. . . you may take it for granted that floating batteries have become elements in amphibious warfare . . . The French no doubt go to great lengths in their praises of this favourite weapon of their Emperor; but make all the allowance you please for that and there will still remain too much in favour of it to admit of its being discarded without fair trial . . .'

The roles had been reversed again decisively: ships could now be made stronger than the new guns.

All the same, the British calmly ignored the lessons of Kinburn. Betwen 1854 and 1856 seventy-three private inventors submitted plans for the construction of shot proof ships but, even so, the only armoured ships built at this time were floating batteries similar to those built by the French. Battleship design remained unchanged. However, in France, the potential of armour had been fully appreciated by at least two men — the Emperor, Napoleon III and a marine designer called Dupuy de Lôme who, on January 1 1857, was appointed *Directeur du Matériel,* a post very similar to that of the British Surveyor of the Navy. De Lôme had been responsible for the design of the excellent French wooden steam battleships which, as we have seen, were so much better than their British counterparts that they began, by 1858, seriously to threaten Britain's supremacy at sea. However, de Lôme now put forward a scheme which was even more revolutionary. Taking one of his most successful designs, the two-decked battleship *Napoléon,* he proposed that a new ship should be built, based on these principal dimensions, but with one gun deck only. The weight saved by losing a deck could then be used to give the ship a complete belt of iron armour plate $4\frac{1}{2}$ inches thick and engines capable of driving her at almost 13 knots. De Lôme's scheme received the full backing of the Emperor and so the famous *Gloire* was born. She was ordered in March 1858, launched on November 29 1859 and was undergoing sea trials by August 1860.

Her arrival heralded a revolution in warship design — but it was not France who actually carried through that revolution. In wooden ship building, once the advent of steam propulsion gave them a chance to start even, the French had been able to hold their own against the British but, as soon as iron ships were introduced, the battle was lost. After all, this was a fight which Britain was uniquely equipped to win at this particular moment in her history.

HMS Caledonia in drydock in Malta 1868
Another of the converted wooden battleships.
In 1867, she was the first ironclad to be appointed
flagship of the Mediterranean fleet

She was far more advanced industrially than her rivals, with private shipyards that were already turning out iron ships by the score and iron smelters whose experience in the art of iron-making was unmatched anywhere else in the world. She had the economic strength that was needed to sustain an arms race based on expensive new technology. And, most important of all, it so happened that at this time both official and public opinion was more than usually prepared to accept heavy expenditure on naval armaments. The threat posed by the French steam battleships had caused another invasion scare in 1858, and the announcement that the *Gloire* was being built made it obvious that some major counter move would have to be made. The Surveyor of the Navy Sir Baldwin Walker, referring to the Admiralty's traditional policy of avoiding any revolutionary changes in the fleet until forced into them by a foreign power, wrote:

' . . . this time has arrived. France has now commenced to build frigates of great speed with their sides protected by thick metal plates and this renders it imperative for this country to do the same without a moment's delay . . .'

At first, the British response was to consider building two wooden iron-clads of similar design to the *Gloire* but soon an even bolder concept began to circulate: nothing less than a huge all-iron ship, with heavy armour plating covering her vital parts. She was to have engines of 5000 hp, which would give her a speed of over 14 knots, despite her size and weight. She was to have a full suit of sails, to enable her to operate anywhere in the world and her unprecedented length of 380 feet and her slender clippership lines meant that, unlike her wooden predecessors, she would perform almost as well under sail as under steam. But her most revolutionary feature, which in fact made her invincible at the time she was launched, was her armament: twenty-six muzzle-loading 68-pounder guns and ten brand-new breech loaders, firing shells of 110 pounds. Her name was to be *Warrior*, but, when they tried to classify her, they found that she would not fit any of the established rates and so were forced to compromise with 'armoured frigate' — thus stretching an already overstrained term too far. Clearly a new word was needed, for everything about her — her size; her iron construction; her watertight compartments; her huge engines and her breech-loading guns — proclaimed that a new age of naval warfare had dawned. And so the word 'ironclad' entered the language.

Historians are all too fond of finding 'watersheds' or 'turning points' but there can be no doubt that December 30 1860, the date of the *Warrior's* launching, was a unique day in naval history. There has never been a moment quite like it, for never before or since has there been a warship which differed so completely from all her predecessors. The *Gloire* had posed a serious threat to the old wooden battleships: the *Warrior* rendered them obsolete at a single stroke. The French ironclad was a clever development of long-established wooden warship design and construction: the *Warrior* was a triumphant assertion of the new skills of iron shipbuilding. British planners had countered the French threat and had also completely changed the face of naval warfare. British industry had risen nobly to the challenge of the new design,

HMS Defence 1862
This 18-gun ironclad was launched in 1861. She was one of the smaller armoured ships built as part of the first ironclad programme

building the revolutionary ship in just over two years from ordering to commissioning — four months *less,* in fact, than it took the French to build the more traditionally-construced *Gloire*! The Admiralty's faith in Britain's industrial ascendency had been amply justified and their cautious policy of the preceding years completely vindicated.

But there was little cause for rejoicing at the time. Although the French card had been decisively trumped, the Admiralty realised that Britain would have to build fast if she were to stay ahead of her rival. And ironclads were extremely expensive. The *Warrior* eventually cost £377,292, while HMS *Undaunted,* a standard wooden screw frigate built at about the same time, cost only £105,00. The Navy Estimates, which had stood at about £9½ million in 1857, rose to well over £12 million in 1860 and 1861. Moreover, a great deal of money, which had been spent only very recently on converting wooden battleships to steam or building new ones, was completely wasted. As a result of the ironclad revolution, very few of the new steam ships served for longer than eight or nine years and the active life of the majority was considerably shorter. The *Duke of Wellington,* the proud flagship of the Baltic Fleet in the campaigns of 1854 and 1855, was taken out of service in 1862, after just nine years in commission, and was converted into a stationary flagship for the Commander-in-Chief, Portsmouth. HMS *Renown* served only one commission in the Mediterranean between 1857 and 1861 before being laid up. The last of the 'wooden walls' ships to fire her guns in anger was HMS *Conqueror* which took part in the Japanese War in 1864; the last to

fly an admiral's flag at sea was HMS *Victoria,* the Mediterranean flagship between 1864 and 1867, and the reign of wooden battleships finally closed in 1870, when HMS *Rodney* paid off in Portsmouth Harbour. In 1858, it looked as if screw propulsion had succeeded in giving another lease of life to these splendid old ships with their towering masts and yards; their tiers of guns and their chequer-board 'Nelson-style' paintwork. Just twelve years later, not one was left in active service and only a few survived as harbour flagships, hulks and accommodation ships. It was a rushed and undignified exit from a stage that they had occupied for so long. As Admiral Sir Henry Codrington said in a debate on the future use of wooden battleships at the Royal United Service Institute in April 1869:

' . . . It has been a heartbreaking thing to officers who have sailed in these ships, and who know them to be as fine ships as were ever built by the hand of man, to see them actually of no use at present and to know that they are being burned in the fires of London . . .'

Never before, or since, has any class of warships been made so completely obsolete so quickly.

Their passing left a void which had to be filled as soon as possible. The French began building sisters to the *Gloire,* or adaptations of her design, as soon as her trials proved successful, but the British proceeded rather more cautiously. The main reason for care was that guns were showing signs of being able once more to penetrate ships' sides — even when protected by the stoutest armour. The introduction of rifling in the gun barrel, which caused the shell to spin, gave far greater accuracy than had been possible with smooth-bores; while the invention of a workable breechloading mechanism by the British armament firm of Armstrong, meant that the new rifled guns could be fired almost as quickly as their predecessors. But all these devices were still experimental. Rifling proved itself time and again, but the breech-loaders were in-efficient and even dangerous. At the bombardment of the Japanese town of Kagoshima on August 15 1863, there were no less than 28 accidents in a squadron that mounted only 21 of the new guns. As a result, the Royal Navy reverted to muzzle-loaders until a more efficient breech mechanism was developed in the 1880s.

However, despite the caution imposed by these experiments, the British shipbuilders began slowly to outstrip their French opponents. The *Warrior* was followed by her near sister the *Black Prince*; by the *Achilles*, the first ironclad built in a royal dockyard; and by the three famous five-masters *Minotaur*, *Agincourt* and *Northumberland*. These six large ships were complemented by five smaller ones which were similar to the *Warrior* in general layout, while differing in such items as speed and armament. But these eleven iron ships were not sufficient on their own to keep Britain ahead of France and so the Admiralty returned to its original plan of building iron-cased wooden ships of a similar design to the *Gloire*. There were nine of these in all; seven were converted two-decker battleships which were cut down by one deck and then armoured. The first, HMS *Royal Oak*, was completed in 1863 and the last, HMS *Repulse*, came into service in 1870. They performed extremely well and to one of them, the *Caledonia*, went the honour of being the first ironclad to be flagship of the Mediterranean fleet in 1867. The other two iron-cased ships, HMS *Lord Warden* and *Lord Clyde* were oddities, since they were new ships, built deliberately of wood in order to use up the large stocks of timber at the Pembroke and Chatham dockyards.

As a result of these measures, the British had 19 ironclads at sea in 1866 compared with 16 French, and the gap continued to widen thereafter. The one advantage that the French possessed was that most of their ships were of similar design so that their fleet was able to operate uniformly; while the British ships had different armaments, speeds and manoeuvring abilities, which made fleet operations difficult. If the two countries had gone to war in the mid-1860s, it is possible that the French might have had the edge. But, in the long run, the British course was the wisest, for in the years following 1860, the development of naval armaments was so rapid that ships very soon became obsolete. A naval architect, Charles Henwood, speaking in the Royal United Services Institute debate of April 1869, said:

'. . . It is universally admitted that there exists at the present time no one type of ship of war which it would be desirable to perpetuate . . . The typical ship on which to found our future Navy has not been built . . .'

That 'typical ship', HMS *Collingwood*, was in fact not destined to be laid down until 1881 and twelve more confused years of fluctuating experimental design lay in between.

HMS Lord Warden leaving Portsmouth Harbour

Launched in 1865, she was one of two wooden ironclads built specially to use up stocks of timber in the Royal dockyards

The launch of HMS Resistance

An 18-gun ironclad, near sister to the Defence, she was launched on April 11, 1861. Most of the ironclads had uniformly black hulls but the Resistance and Defence were given a traditional white strake during their first commissions

The transitional fleet 1863

The Channel squadron in 1863, when the change-over
from wooden to armoured ships was half completed.
On the right are the ironclads led by HMS Warrior.
On the left is the flagship, HMS Edgar, a 91-gun
wooden screw battleship

The new Navy 1869
The combined Channel and Mediterranean fleets
on joint exercises at Gibraltar in September 1869.
The Admiralty Board is embarked in HMS Agincourt
on the left — the distinctive Admiralty Board
flag with its horizontal anchor can be seen
flying from her main mast

Gunboats

Almost the only new development in small ship design between 1830 and 1870 was the re-introduction of especially designed classes of gunboats in 1854. Intended specifically to counter the massive Russian fortresses in the Baltic and Black Seas, these small, shallow-draught vessels were armed with two or three heavy guns. In fact the Crimean War ended before many of the gunboats were in full service. However, all were not wasted. Some were sent out to China, where they proved ideal for river warfare

Ironclads under full sail 1869

In the foreground is HMS Inconstant, a 16-gun unarmoured iron frigate. Astern of her is the ironclad Royal Oak

Gunboat of the Dapper Class at Spithead 1856

In all, 118 gunboats of this class alone were built between February 1855 and June 1856. It was a massive effort which demonstrated just how strong were Britain's shipbuilding capabilities

51

Gunboat tactics

Gunboats were designed to fight at close ranges, relying on their small size and manoeuvreability to protect them from enemy fire, while their heavy guns enabled them to land powerful blows. The mother battleships would give long-range covering fire as the boats went into attack (above) and they would then anchor in widely dispersed groups to give the enemy as wide a target as possible (below)

HMS Colossus and her division of gunboats at Spithead 1856

Gunboats were organised into divisions which were each attached to a battleship. These acted as mother ships — providing the gunboat crews with stores and permanent accommodation since there was usually little room for either in the tiny hulls

Gunboats setting sail for China 1857

In the foreground is HMS Furious, a 16-gun paddle frigate, which acted as escort for this particular detachment of gunboats

HMS Furious and her charges at Madeira, 1857

On the right are two gunboats of the Clown class (two guns, 40 hp engines). They have been specially fitted with square sails on their foremasts to enable them to make the arduous voyage half across the world

Gunboats in action at Escape Creek, 1857

In the foreground are the gunboats Starling and Staunch. Both of the Dapper class, they had been transferred to the China station earlier in the year

55

The Social Revolution
The great technological changes of the period 1830 -70
were matched by social innovations which were, in their way,
just as revolutionary. Gradually, the Royal Navy ceased to be a
part-time, haphazard organisation and became a full-time
professional force

The main deck of a warship c 1830
Shore leave was seldom granted at this period
— even in peacetime. Sailors were left to organise
their own amusements such as gambling, and
women were 'imported' in abundance

The new professionals

THE GREAT TECHNOLOGICAL CHANGE^S of 1830-1870 were matched by social developments which were, in their way, just as revolutionary. In 1830, the personnel of the fleet were still distinctly Nelsonian: by 1870, both they and the conditions in which they lived had become recognisably modern. Indeed, some of the most important features of today's Navy, which are now taken for granted — such as continuous service, a retired list for officers, uniforms for ratings, pensions, medals, reserves and training establishments — all date from this period.

The Officers

In 1830, the great problem facing most naval officers was unemployment. At the end of the Great War, the Navy had been severely reduced — from 713 ships in commission in 1814 to a peace establishment of 134 by 1820 — and this figure remained fairly constant during the first half of the nineteenth century. As a result, of the 5797 active officers on the Navy List in 1818, only 597 were actually employed — a beggarly 10.3 per cent. The problem was made worse by the fact that, at this time, no proper system of retirement existed. Once an officer had reached the rank of Post Captain, he continued to rise slowly up the Navy List, whether he was in active service or not, until he died. As a result, promotion was extremely slow — literally a system of filling 'dead men's shoes' — and by the 1840s and 1850s, the average age of the senior officers was extremely high. Sir Robert Stopford, who commanded at the Bombardment of Acre in 1840, was 72 and, in 1854, when the Crimean War broke out, the choice for the important Baltic Command lay between three men. Lord

Theatricals on board HMS Perseus in Yokohama Bay, Japan 1864

By this time, shore leave was beginning to be regarded as a right rather than a privilege and sailors were encouraged to pursue 'improving' pastimes — reading and writing and, as seen here, amateur theatricals

57

Dundonald (who, as Thomas Cochrane, had been one of the most famous naval personalities of the Great War) was rejected, not because of his age (79), but because he was considered too reckless! Sir John Ommaney, who had been a Captain at Navarino in 1827, and was then Commander-in-Chief, Plymouth at the age of 81, nearly got the job, but unfortunately fell ill from the extra strain caused by getting all the ships at Plymouth ready for sea. And Sir Charles Napier, who was eventually chosen, was 68 years old! The system also meant that it was perfectly possible for a man to become an admiral, and even to fly his flag at sea, without having held any important commands as a captain. Perhaps the saddest example was Rear-Admiral David Price, who commanded a British squadron in the Pacific at the outbreak of the Crimean War. He had a brilliant career during the Great War, rising to the rank of Captain in 1815, but there had then followed 39 soul-destroying years as he crawled up the captain's list, with only a brief spell in command of a 50-gun ship, and as a commissioner of a dockyard to relieve the strain. On 30 August 1854, his squadron sailed to the Russian port of Petropavlovsk, to attack enemy ships that were based there but, even as his ships were going into attack, Price went below and shot himself. Nothing in his previous career had prepared him for the loneliness and strain of commanding a detached squadron many thousands of miles from home.

The Admiralty was aware that this antiquated system prevented the promotion of bright young men but their lordships' hands were tied by the old-fashioned views of the officers themselves. At this time, the only distinction between an officer on active service and an officer ashore was that the latter received only half his annual salary. Indeed, the common term to describe his situation was 'on half pay'. In 1847, the Admiralty made an important step towards clearing the blockage by persuading 200 super-annuated captains to accept promotion to flag-rank (and therefore an increase in their half pay!) in return for relinquishing their right to be considered for active service postings. This step was formalised in 1851 by the creation of a special category of officer — namely those who were said to be 'On Reserve Half Pay' — and so the modern concept of Officers RN (Rtd) was born. The system worked well and, by 1865, the blockage was clearing fast. In January 1842, there were 709 'active' captains on the list and only 105 of them were employed. By 1865, the active number had been reduced to the more realistic figure of 297 and, of these, 134 were employed. A career in the peacetime Navy was becoming more of a full-time affair than ever before.

At the same time, a naval officer's career was becoming more specialised. For centuries, the various non-military tasks in warships had been performed by special officers who were appointed by a warrant from the Navy Board — the organisation which dealt with the 'business' side of the Navy. These officers — the Purser (who supervised a ship's stores), the Master (who was in charge of navigation), the Chaplain and the Surgeon — all lived in the Wardroom with the lieutenants and Royal Marine officers, but they were a race apart from the 'commissioned' officers, who concerned themselves above all with the fighting and sailing of the ship. Gradually however, as the Navy became more complex and

59

Sailor's woollen embroidery c 1860

The making of brightly coloured, framed embroideries, adorned with flags and ships, was a popular way of passing the time in the Victorian Navy

The midshipmen's mess by Cruikshank c 1835

In the old sailing warships, the senior midshipmen lived in a mess on the Orlop deck, which was below the waterline and just above the hold

The wardroom of HMS Duke of Wellington 1855

A celebration dinner is in progress in honour of Admiral Dundas, the C-in-C, Baltic. The large wooden steam battleships were so comfortable that there was opposition in the service when they began to be replaced by the more cramped ironclads

modernised, the specialised tasks became more important and so the functions of the old warrant officers began to be exercised by fully organised departments or 'branches' — and, eventually, the heads of those departments became commissioned officers. Thus, by 1870, it was possible for a new officer entrant to have a choice of career: either he could become an ordinary seaman officer; or he could specialise as a surgeon, a paymaster (secretary), navigator, instructor or — most striking of all — as an engineer.

The specialist branches had to struggle to obtain both recognition by the Naval Establishment and commissions for their senior officers — but none more so than the engineers. As we have already seen, the earliest engineers were simply mechanics sent aboard by the firm which fitted the engines and the obvious place to house them was with the sailors. However, as steam gained an increasing foothold in the warships of the Navy during the 1830s, so it was acknowledged that a properly organised branch of naval engineers was needed to man these new steamships. In 1836, the Engineer Branch was formed and its senior officers were appointed by warrants from the Navy Board. All the same, they were not considered worthy of wardroom rank and were placed among the lesser Warrant Officers, such as the carpenter or boatswain, which meant that they lived in tiny cabins of their own — usually on the orlop deck, which was below the waterline. There is no doubt at all that this treatment of the engineers was inspired largely by snobbery and conservatism — an attitude summed up best by a splendidly patronising remark attributed to Admiral Sir George Cockburn:

The gunroom of HMS Caesar 1855
The large wooden steam battleships of the 1850s
were much roomier than their predecessors, with
more headroom between decks

Signal for an engagement abroad
One of a pair of popular engravings published by J Fairburn in
1838 (See also engraving on Page 2). Note the sailor's
fashionably tight trousers and the elaborate sideburns and
ringlets — obviously his 'Sunday best'. At this time there was no
official uniform so sailors were free to improvise

' . . . Since the introduction of the steam vessel I have never seen a
clean deck, or a Captain who, when he calls upon me, does not
look like a sweep . . .'
Gradually however, such attitudes were overcome — although
traces of them were to last even until the early twentieth century.
In 1843, the senior warrant officers — the pursers, chaplains and
surgeons — became commissioned officers but the engineers had
to wait for four more years until they gained their coveted
commissions and were allowed at last into the wardroom. As a
result, men of better experience and of higher social standing
began to join the Navy as engineers and these, in their turn,
improved the image of the branch. Indeed, some aspiring young
seaman officers began deliberately to acquire specialised
knowledge of steamships, recognising that their career prospects
would be considerably enhanced if they did so. One such was
Astley Cooper Key, later First Sea Lord who, in January 1844, took
the remarkable step of asking to be transferred from HMS *Curacoa*,
a crack 24-gun sailing frigate on detached service under a popular
captain, to HMS *Gorgon*, an early 6-gun paddleship. It was a brave
move to make, at a time when 'steamer lieutenant' was still a term
of abuse in many wardrooms, but in fact it turned out very well.
Key wrote home:
' . . . Being in a steamer has given me a much greater interest in the
service than I had before, from having, I suppose, an object in view
to which I feel myself suited . . . '
and the move also helped his career, for he remained constantly
employed afloat between 1844 and 1859, and always in the new

Upper yard men of HMS Phoebe 1864
The men are all wearing the new 1857 uniform (see next page).
Note how shapeless it is compared with the 'unofficial' rig of the
amorous sailor on this page. Note also that the sailors are all
barefooted. This gave them a better grip than shoes when

Captain John Ommaney

The captain of HMS Albion at the Battle of Navarino, 1827. He is wearing the 1833 pattern uniform with red facings on the collar and cuffs, introduced by order of William IV. Officers' uniforms of the 1830s still looked very Nelsonian as this contemporary print on the right clearly shows. First-class volunteers were equivalent to modern cadets; second-class volunteers were trainee masters

The waiting room at the Admiralty 1835

64

The main problem facing many officers in 1830 was unemployment. In the much-reduced peacetime Navy, appointments afloat were in very short supply. This caricature by Cruikshank shows unemployed officers in the Admiralty waiting room in search of postings

Sailor's uniform 1857

In 1853 continuous service replaced the old 'hire and fire' system of employing sailors and so for the first time, the Navy became a truly full-time occupation. As a result, a single uniform was designed for the whole service. The first official sailors' uniform was introduced in 1857

steamships, which were fast coming into service during these years. Key was an early example of the modern type of specialist officer who owes the success of his career to his recognised abilities in a clearly defined field.

One final change which had an important effect upon the naval officers of our period, was the growth of formal training for new entrants. Traditionally, officers had gone to sea as young teenagers, usually in the ship of a relative or patron and had learned their trade very largely by trial and error. Nelson, as is well known, had been taken to sea at the age of twelve by his uncle, Captain Maurice Suckling. It was realised that this sytem was too haphazard, and that the success of the new entrant depended too much upon 'interest' — in other words, on whom he knew! In an attempt to combat this unfairness and to introduce a more uniform system of entry, the Royal Naval Academy had been founded in Portsmouth Dockyard. However, the Academy — or College as it was later called — had a very chequered career and there was a great deal of prejudice within the Navy against 'college volunteers'. Moreover, during the 1820s, a specialist branch of naval schoolmasters began to evolve and, by 1830, most large ships had at least one schoolmaster aboard. In 1836, they became wardroom officers appointed by warrant and in 1840 they were given the title 'schoolmasters and instructors' which later became simply 'instructor'. As a result, it was felt that the best place for young officers to learn their trade was, once again, at sea and so in 1837 the College ceased to take new entrants and, thereafter, all initial training was done afloat.

Naval officers' uniforms 1856

In April 1856 a new pattern of officers uniforms was introduced which was recognisably modern. The ranks are (left to right): Lieutenant, Captain, Admiral and Midshipman. At this time, Lieutenants had only one ring and Captains three. The extra rings were added in 1861 when the rank of Sub-lieutenant was first introduced

The officers of HMS Phoebe 1864

Victorian officers never really looked as smart as the
fashion plates suggest. Several different combinations of
uniforms were permitted for daily wear and the
result was often suprisingly scruffy! Note how casual
and relaxed are the officers in this picture. The
Captain is in fact the man seated centre with his
cap at a jaunty angle!

However, in 1854, a training ship, HMS *Illustrious* was established in Portsmouth Harbour to receive young naval ratings for their introduction to the Navy. The experiment succeeded and her captain, Robert Harris, decided that the system would work equally well with trainee officers. He therefore set his son to work with the ratings and the Admiralty was so pleased with the young man's progress that, in 1857, they inaugurated a completely new scheme for the education and examination of all new officer entrants — who were now called naval cadets. The scheme was started in the *Illustrious* and soon displaced the training of the young ratings, who were moved elsewhere. In 1858, the *Illustrious* was replaced by an old three-decker *Britannia* and this famous name was retained by all the ships used for this purpose thereafter.

So, by 1870, all new officer entrants to the Navy were given uniform training and had to pass a uniform examination before proceeding to active service afloat. Thanks to the new retirement measures, which had significantly reduced the number of active officers, they had a good chance of remaining in full employment throughout their careers. And the growth of specialist branches meant that men were able to develop their particular gifts in the certain knowledge that specialisation would assist their promotion. The Royal Navy was losing the rather exclusive 'gentlemanly' image of its earlier years and was becoming much more of a profession.

The men

The growth of professionalism among the officers was matched by similar trends on the lower deck. Whereas there had always been too many officers, there were never sufficient sailors available. And yet, in fact, there should have been no shortage of suitable men, for Britain was a predominantly maritime nation with a large pool of seafarers at her disposal. The difficulty lay in persuading them to join up for war service. Contrary to all the romantic stories that are still told about them, the notorious Press Gangs had very seldom wasted their time with inexperienced landsmen. Their main purpose had been to compel seafaring men to join the Navy and most of their efforts had been concentrated in ports and fishing villages. They had succeeded in obtaining the necessary men but, not suprisingly, they were extremely unpopular and, although the enabling legislation remained on the Statute Book, they were never used again after 1815 — not even at the outbreak of the Crimean War in 1854. Both the Admiralty and the officers accepted that men had to be persuaded to volunteer to join the Navy and, as a result, most of the social changes of this period were designed to make the service a more attractive career.

One of the main complaints against service in the Navy had been its uncertainty. The Army has been made a standing force in 1661 and the Royal Marines became a regular corps in 1775. However, even as late at 1830, the Navy was still not a permanent body. Only the lesser warrant officers — the boatswain, the gunner and the carpenter — were employed without interruption, since their skills were needed whether the ship was in full service or merely in reserve. Commissioned officers, as we have seen, usually spent long periods ashore on half pay in between appointments. And the sailors were signed on for one commission only and, at the end of that commission, they could easily find themselves unemployed — the 'hire and fire' system. There were no barracks where they could be housed in between ships and no guarantees of future employment, unless another ship happened to be short of hands.

The first step towards developing a full-time Navy came in 1830, when the new gunnery training vessel, HMS *Excellent*, was first commissioned at Portsmouth. It had been set up as a result of pressure from gunnery experts who believed that the Navy would benefit greatly if a uniform system of gunnery drill was introduced and, despite initial opposition, it was in fact remarkably successful and soon established a reputation as the main centre for scientific investigation into new weapons and drill. But for our story, it is one of *Excellent*'s side-effects that is important. For, realising that it would be foolish to spend money in training sailors if their future service was uncertain, the Admiralty decided that any seaman joining the *Excellent* should be engaged for a minimum of five or seven years and that this engagement should be renewable, with an increase of pay on each occasion. Moreover, to induce the seaman to undergo this new training, they approved an extra allowance of two shillings (10 new pence) a month for every man who qualified. So, for the first time, men were being encouraged to look upon the Navy as a permanent career instead of casual work.

This development at *Excellent* began a trend towards long term service which continued throughout the period 1830-70. In 1846, the Admiralty issued an order which empowered officers to allow men a month or six weeks paid leave at the end of a commission, after which they could join another ship of their choice at any port. Moreover, their hammocks and clothes could be stored in the dockyard to await their return. In 1853, came the most significant step of all. All boy entrants were to be signed on for ten years ' . . . continuous and general service . . .' beginning at the age of 18 and HMS *Illustrious* was set aside as a training ship so that they could be properly prepared for their new career. The old rate of 'landsman' (which, as it implies, had meant an inexperienced man) was abolished and a new higher rate of 'Leading Seaman' was established between Able Seaman and Petty Officer. Additionally, another new rate of Chief Petty officer was introduced, thus giving the lower deck a complete hierarchy which was comparable to that of the commissioned officers and which offered more opportunities to an ambitious man. The scheme worked well and 'Jemmy Graham's Novices' as they were called (after the First Lord who introduced the idea) slowly worked their way through the service until, by 1870, there were hardly any 'hire and fire' sailors left.

Although these measures went a long way towards providing a solid nucleus of permanent peace-time sailors, they did little to ease the problem of manning the Navy in time of war. An early step towards a solution came in 1835 when the first Merchant Shipping Act provided for the drawing up of a Register of Seamen. The idea was that all men who earned their livings by

The specialists

Another important social development of this period was the growth of specialist branches within the Navy, each with its own hierarchy of commissioned officers. These replaced the old warrant officers of the Nelsonian period such as the surgeons, pursers and masters

Chaplain taking divine service in HMS Caesar 1855

The Reverend Joseph Smithland, Chaplain of HMS Caesar, leading prayers. Like many of his fellow-chaplains, he was a qualified naval instructor, responsible for the education of all the midshipmen in the Caesar

seafaring should be put on a list so that, in wartime, they could be called upon in batches to serve for periods of up to five years. However, prejudice against the Navy was still very strong among merchant seamen and the scheme never really worked. The problem continued to exercise the minds both of the Admiralty and of serving officers and a number of pamphlets and articles putting forward ingenious solutions were written at this time. In 1847, Lieutenant J H Brown suggested that a voluntary naval reserve should be formed and this idea actually got as far as Parliament before being rejected. Meanwhile, the French caused considerable concern in 1851 by publishing figures showing that they had 16,000 men in active service, and a further 48,500 trained men in their Merchant Service who were liable for call-up in the event of a war. The situation was further aggravated in 1854 when the fleet was mobilised for the Crimean War. Although the Register of Seamen had more than 250,000 names on it, a mere 400 men volunteered for war service and the ships of the Baltic fleet had to be brought up to complement by employing elderly coastguards, and even by hiring Scandinavian sailors!

As a result of this fiasco, a special Royal Commission was appointed in 1858 to enquire into the manning of the Navy and, this time, J H Brown's scheme received full official endorsement. Its most important feature was that it was to be a *voluntary* system but, at the same time, the reservists were to be eligible for the same pay, pensions and allowances that were payable to long-service men in similar rates. Special drill ships were established for reservists at certain key ports throughout the country; annual

Dispensary on board HMS Melbourne

With the growth of a properly organised medical branch, care of the sick improved considerably in the Navy; special foods and above all, hospital ships such as the Melbourne all improved the sailor's chances of recovery

cruises were arranged and, perhaps most important of all, training ships — such as the famous *Worcester* and *Conway* — were set up under the aegis of the Board of Trade to prepare boys for careers in the merchant service and, if needed, in the Royal Navy. The new scheme started slowly but, in November 1861, at the outset of the American Civil War, a British mail ship was stopped and boarded by a Northern US warship which was searching for Southern diplomats. This incident caused widespread outrage in Britain and, as a direct result, by spring 1862, 12,000 men had enrolled in the new Royal Naval Reserve. Thereafter, the reserve was firmly established.

These important reforms were supplemented by a more generous and enlightened attitude towards the rewards of service. A sailor's pay had always been a strong cause of contention; indeed, one of the main reasons why merchant seamen were so reluctant to join the Navy was that the pay was so much lower than they were used to. Gradually, however, the pay was raised until by 1870 an Able Seaman was earning 49s 1d (£2.45½) a month which, together with the extra allowances for special skills and good conduct which he could now earn, made his total wage almost twice that of his counterpart in 1830. Another source of grievance had been that the wages were always paid in one lump sum at the *end* of a commission — which invariably lasted three years, and often more. Thus, a sailor had no means of providing for his family during his long absences, and they had to survive until his ship returned — a date that could never be predicted accurately. The obvious answer to this problem was for a proportion of the men's pay to be forwarded to their families at regular intervals, and such a scheme required a great deal of extra paperwork. However, the ideal persons for such work already existed — the pursers, who hitherto had been responsible solely for the ships' stores. In 1825, they were allowed for the first time to handle a small proportion of the total wages and, in 1842 their title was changed to 'Purser and Paymaster'. Finally, in 1851, they were given responsibility for the regular payment of all wages and so the old 'paying off' ceremony at the end of each commission, followed by the inevitable drunken debauch ashore, became an event of the past.

There were similar advances in the payment of pensions. Awards had been given for wounds and some elderly sailors had been cared for in Greenwich Hospital, in exactly the same way as the modern Chelsea pensioners, since 1705. But places in the hospital were limited and so, in 1831, the authorities began to issue out-pensions to petty officers and seamen who had been discharged because of wounds incurred while serving in the Navy. Eventually, in 1869, these out-pensions completely replaced the hospital, which was closed down. Also, in 1830, a long service grant was introduced for seamen and marines who were being discharged after serving for 21 years or more. It was decided that this award should be marked by some tangible gift and so the first naval Long Service and Good Conduct Medal was authorised on July 19 1830.

The modern concept of using specially-produced, named medals

Chaplain taking prayers on board a China gunboat
A chaplain's 'parish' was seldom confined to one ship, and he had widely dispersed ships under his care

to reward war service was also largely a Victorian innovation. During the Great War, senior officers had received special gold medals for certain notable actions and the battles of the Nile and Trafalgar had been commemorated by the award of medals to every participant. However, these latter had been paid for by private individuals, and the metal from which the medals were made varied from gold to pewter, according to the rank of the recipient! Nonetheless, the concept of identical campaign medals for all was growing. The Honourable East India Company had a tradition, dating back to 1784, of awarding medals to all its armed forces — including native troops — and, in 1842, it decided to issue a medal for service in the First China War (1840-42). A number of regular Army and Navy units had also taken part and the British Government realised that these should receive some reward as well. Accordingly, in 1843, it decided to issue the First China War Medal itself. It was made of silver in a uniform size, suspended from a coloured ribbon, with the recipient's name engraved round the edge — in short, the first modern campaign medal.

Once the precedent had been established, people pointed out the anomaly that a comparatively minor war should be so lavishly rewarded, when the service of many thousands of men in the Great War of 1793-1815 were still, largely, unrecognised. Much public discussion ensued — including debates in Parliament — and eventually, in 1847, the first Naval General Service Medal was instituted with special clasps to cover 231 selected actions of varying importance between 1793 and 1840. A similar medal was

produced for the Army and, thereafter, the basic concept of
campaign medals remained unchanged — although the actual
form that they took altered according to the conditions of the times
and the type of war which they were commemorating.

The early Victorian period also saw the introduction of gallantry
medals. The first was the Meritorious Service Medal of 1849 which,
although intended primarily for the Army, was also given to a few
Royal Marine sergeants. In 1855, the Conspicuous Gallantry
Medal was introduced for naval ratings and Royal Marines, but
this lasted for only a few months before being overtaken in January
1856 by the most famous award of all — the Victoria Cross. This
decoration, which was first awarded retrospectively for acts of
gallantry during the Crimean War, was truly democratic — officers
and men alike of both services were eligible and the actual cross
was exactly the same, whatever the rank of the recipient. Indeed,
its dull, bronze colour made it the least ostentatious of all the
gallantry awards, and it was rendered even more inconspicuous
by the fact that, until 1918, it was worn on a red ribbon by Army
recipients, and on a blue ribbon by Naval personnel, so that it
tended to blend into their uniforms. But there was seldom
anything inconspicuous about the manner in which it was
presented. The first ceremony took place at a grand parade in
Hyde Park on June 27 1857, when the Queen pinned the new
decoration to the chests of sixty Crimean War heroes, including
twelve naval recipients, in front of a crowd of more than 100,000.
The senior naval officer on parade, and therefore the first man ever
to receive his VC, was Commander Henry Raby who, together

**Naval Engineer's Medal awarded
to William Dunkin 1842**

The newest branch of all was the engineering branch.
The engineers had a long struggle to obtain recognition
and in 1842, when this medal was awarded, their senior
officers were still only appointed by warrant. They
did not receive commissions until 1847

Captain Astley Cooper Key

Cooper Key had the foresight to specialise in steam as early as 1844 — at a time when 'steamer lieutenant' was still a term of abuse in many wardrooms. His decision helped his career, for he remained almost constantly employed afloat

with two fellow-sailors, had rescued a wounded soldier from the No Man's Land outside Sebastopol. He had done this without receiving a single scratch, despite heavy enemy fire — but family tradition claims that he did have to lose *some* blood to obtain his Cross, for the Queen pinned it right into his chest. Needless to say, he never flinched! Queen Victoria continued to take a close personal interest in 'her' decoration and insisted on presenting it herself whenever possible. And, even if she was unable to do so, a VC presentation was always a very grand affair, usually held in public with full military honours. In this way the intention expressed in the original Royal Warrant was fulfilled: namely, that the new award ' . . . should be highly prized and eagerly sought after by the officers and men of our Naval and Military Services . . . '

As a result of all these extra inducements, a naval career was becoming a more attractive proposition by 1870. John Bechervaise, a seaman who had experienced the full rigours of the old navy, wrote, as early as 1847:

' . . . the system of manning ships has improved with the march of intellect; and men who join the Navy, in nine cases out of ten, gladly remain until they are promoted, or get pensions, perhaps medals for long service and good conduct . . . '

Indeed, he heartily approved of the new medal:

' . . . Among the various changes introduced since the Peace, for the benefit of seamen of the Royal Navy, there is not one that has been so useful, or tended to so much good, as the medal and gratuity money given for long service and good conduct . . . '

Training

The growth of well organised training of both officers and men was an important feature of the Victorian social revolution in the Navy. It raised the standard of personnel of all ranks

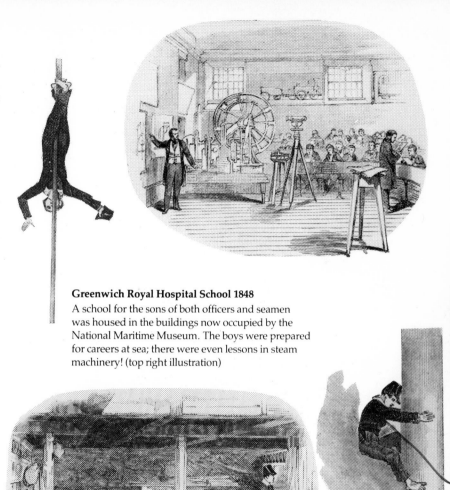

So, steadily, the type of man entering the Navy began to change. Gone forever was the rough, foul-mouthed sailor of countless songs and drawings. The man who had taken his place was better educated, more literate and far more reliable. He was no angel, certainly, and his antics ashore still tended to be on the debauched side by contemporary landsman's standards. But, even so, the new sailors were becoming very popular. As we shall see, their exploits in the many colonial campaigns of the period captured the public imagination and, as a result, entertainments with nautical themes were always successful. Actors such as T P Cooke — who had himself fought at the Battle of St. Vincent in 1797 — became famous for their portrayal of sailors in plays such as 'Black Ey'd Susan', 'Poor Jack' or 'The Ocean of Life.' Indeed, it is not going too far to say that, at this time, sailors were folk heroes — very much as cowboys or space travellers are today.

Conditions

Despite all these changes in status and rewards, it is doubtful if the Navy would have bcome such a popular career if basic living conditions had not changed so completely as well. If the quality of the men making up the average ship's company was so much higher in 1870 than in 1830, it was obvious that these men would have to be treated differently. A classic example of this truism was the changing attitude to flogging. During the Great War flogging had been justified by the fact that a large proportion of the crews had been made up of Quota Men — petty criminals who had been offered the choice between service in the Navy or prison. There is plenty of evidence to suggest that the professional sailors accepted

Greenwich Royal Hospital School 1848
A school for the sons of both officers and seamen was housed in the buildings now occupied by the National Maritime Museum. The boys were prepared for careers at sea; there were even lessons in steam machinery! (top right illustration)

Model frigate, 1848
An Illustrated London News engraving showing
the model frigate soon after it was constructed

that flogging was necessary to keep these unruly elements under control — for example, there was no mention of flogging in the sailors' demands made during the Great Mutiny of 1797. However, after the war, when there were no longer any quota men, opinion both inside and, most important, outside the Navy began to change. The question was debated in Parliament, and the *United Service Magazine* began publishing flogging returns from ships, criticising those that they thought excessive. Enlightened captains introduced tables of alternative punishments and gradually the number of offences for which a man could be flogged was reduced until finally, in 1871, flogging was 'suspended in peacetime'. Eight years later, it was 'suspended in wartime' and, in typical British fashion, it remains so to this day — not abolished, but *suspended!*

One of the main reasons for the excessive amount of flogging in the old navy was drunkenness — which was hardly surprising, bearing in mind that a man's daily ration of rum was half a pint! Admittedly, this was watered down to make 'grog' in a ratio of 50:50 but, even so, it was a very potent ration indeed. Nonetheless, the Admiralty was afraid that mutiny would break out if the amount was reduced, and so it was not until 1825 that the first step towards a more sensible allowance was taken and the ration was reduced by a half. In 1850, it was halved again and, at about the same time, regular supplies of tea and cocoa were offered in lieu of spirits to those who preferred them. To the Admiralty's amazement, many sailors took the beverages and there was no serious trouble over the reduction in spirits. The point was, of course, that neither flogging, nor excessive amounts of alcohol were needed any longer: the old jail-birds had disappeared and they had been replaced by responsible, professional men.

These adjustments were matched by other smaller, but equally positive changes. Libraries were sanctioned for sea-going ships in 1838 and John Bechervaise noted in 1847 how this had '. . . more powerfully tended to improve the minds of seamen that can be supposed . . .' He could recall days when a book was such a rarity on the lower deck that, if a mess had one, it was read and re-read so often that it became difficult to tell the original colour.

'. . . How different it is now; every one can get a book and read for himself . . . We have men now in the service, and I could name more than twenty from one ship, who, on entering into her did not know one letter in the book; and now, within five years, have learnt how to read and write and cypher merely at their spare time . . .'

The ships' menu was also made more varied, including pressed meat instead of the old 'salt horse'; proper bread, instead of the old weevil-ridden biscuits, and regular supplies of fresh vegetables. Fresh water was more readily available, thanks to the installation of iron tanks, which preserved the water better than the old wooden casks, and the introduction of distilling apparatus in ships fitted with steam engines. Savings banks for sailors and Royal Marines were established in 1866, and the Royal Portsmouth Sailors' Home, which first opened in 1851, offered beds and other club facilities to sailors on shore leave, thus keeping them off the streets and out of the pubs and brothels. Care of the sick improved

77

Model frigate at Greenwich c 1900
A 'frigate' was specially constructed in the grounds
of the school at Greenwich on board which the boys
could learn sail-handling and gunnery

immeasurably, with the provision of properly equipped sick bays
and the appointment in 1833 of special ratings to assist the Surgeon
who were known as 'Sick berth attendants'. Finally, and perhaps
most important of all, an official uniform for ratings was
introduced in 1857. This was largely the result of the decision to
encourage long-service in 1853 — now, at last, it had become
practical to issue clothes of good quality to the seamen, in the
knowledge that they would remain in the service for at least ten
years. It was a significant step. Before 1857, the dress of the sailors
had been largely dependent upon the individual whim of the
captain of the ship in which they were serving. Now, the whole
service was uniformly dressed, reflecting the growing uniformity
in recruitment, training, pay, pensions and diet.

All the same, it would be wrong to view the Navy of 1870 in too
rosy a light. Life afloat was still very hard, although the changes we
have noted at least made it a little less brutal and cruel. Perhaps the
last word is best left to three men who speak from personal
experience. The first is Admiral George Ballard, who joined the
Navy in 1875 and survived to write a definitive series of articles on
the mid-Victorian Navy in the *Mariner's Mirror* between 1929 and
1952:

'. . . The bare bleakness of the mess-deck with its long range of
plank tables had as little suggestion of physical ease as a prison cell.
It was damp and chilly in a cold climate and damp and hot in the
tropics. It was swept by searching draughts if the ports were open,
and nearly pitch dark if they were closed, glass scuttles not having
been invented. It was dimly lit at night by tallow candles inside

Training on board HMS Britannia 1859

Training for officer cadets started on board HMS Illustrious in 1857 and was transferred to the larger Britannia in 1858. Moored originally in Portsmouth Harbour, she was moved to Portland and eventually to Dartmouth, where the training of officers continues to this day — but nowadays on shore

lamps at long intervals, and as there were no drying rooms it reeked of wet serge and flannel in rainy weather. In short, the living quarters of the mid-Victorian bluejacket, stoker, or marine were as widely dissociated from any ideal of home as could well be imagined.

'Moreover, he was always in a crowd by day or night. His work and his leisure, his eating, drinking, washing and sleeping were all in crowded surroundings. He swallowed his bully beef and hard tack, his pea soup, 'copper rattle', and rum, at a mess table so congested that he had absolutely no elbow room and scarce space to sit. He washed himself twice a week on deck at the same time as he washed his clothes, in the two tubfuls of cold water which formed the allowance for the whole twenty five men in his mess, in the middle of a splashing mob at other tubs all round; and he slung his hammock nightly among hundreds of others so tightly packed that they had no swinging room however much the ship rolled. Even in the head he had no privacy . . .'

And yet, here is John Bechervaise's conclusion to his book:

'. . . I only wish to point out to those with whom I have spent so many comfortable days, the benefits offered in the Navy; as well as to assure them that I look back with sincere pleasure after a long period of service, to the day in which I entered it . . .'

And another sailor, Thomas Holman, who joined in 1872, wrote in his memoirs twenty years later:

'. . . I now have to answer the question whether we should send our boys to the Navy. I say *Yes*, emphatically *Yes* — after a period of twenty years in the lower ranks. My school contemporaries may now be a bit ahead of me, but I doubt if many of them have extracted so much fun and enjoyment out of the last twenty years of life as I have done; I am quite certain none of them have been happier or are more in love with their profession . . .'

Visit of the Prince of Wales to the training ship Worcester 1866

Training for both the Royal Navy and Merchant Navy became common as the century progressed. The Worcester, a 52-gun frigate, launched in 1843, was handed over in 1862 for service as a training ship on the Thames

HMS Excellent in Portsmouth Harbour c 1840

Besides training new entrants, the Navy also started specialised training for officers and seamen of all ranks. The first such establishment was the gunnery school in HMS Excellent, started in 1830

Sailors at gunnery drill c 1850

The sailors who joined the Excellent were appointed for a renewable term of at least five or seven years. This was the first system of continuous employment in the history of the Royal Navy

'Hurrah for the life of a sailor'

The old, rather disreputable image of the sailor was fading. The new-look profession was attracting a much more respectable type of man than before, and the seamen's exploits in the many colonial wars of the period captured the public imagination. Songs, books and plays all reflected the sailors' popularity. Indeed they were becoming folk-heroes — rather like the cowboys or space travellers today

The sailor-actor

T P Cooke was a sailor turned actor who made a name for himself by portraying sailors on the stage. He had served as a Boy Third Class in HMS Raven in the Battle of St Vincent in 1797, which entitled him to this Naval General Service medal (above) issued in 1848. He is wearing the medal in the adjacent engraving

On stage
T P Cooke is seen portraying Ben Backstay

Staffordshire pottery figure of T P Cooke
Cooke became so famous that pottery figures were made of him dancing a hornpipe in another of his roles — a sailor called Fid. The figure was based on a drawing made for some 'Penny Plain Twopence Coloured' theatrical plates

Scene from the play 'Black Ey'd Susan'
Cooke's most famous role was Sweet William, a sailor in the play 'Black Ey'd Susan'. He played the part many times in the course of his career

Scene from a nautical melodrama 'The Port Admiral' 1863

Plays with a nautical theme were always popular during the Victorian period. This play, described as 'a subaquaeous, ultramarine, aquario-domestic drama', was performed at a charity fete in aid of the Royal Hospital for Incurables

Jack and the Chinaman — Magic Lantern Show 1858

This slide show, given at a children's Christman party by a gentlemen with the suspicious name of 'Professor Smiley', capitalises on the exploits of the naval brigades in China

Captain Frederick Marryat

Captain Marryat entered the Navy in 1806, saw service in the Great War and was senior naval officer during the opening stages of the First Burma war (1824-26). He made his name as a novelist because of his books about the sea such as 'Mr Midshipman Easy' and 'Masterman Ready'

In order to make the Navy a more attractive career, much attention was paid during the Victorian period to the rewards of service such as pay and pensions. In particular, the awarding of medals for long service, war service or gallantry was developed. Medals as we know them today originated in the period 1830-70

Visitor's Day c 1870

The growing popularity of the Navy was reflected in the desire of people to visit RN ships and see round them. Cruises by ships of the Channel fleet to the ports of Britain became annual events. Here, a smartly-dressed holiday crowd throngs the upper deck of one of the great five-masted ironclads — probably HMS Minotaur

Greenwich Pensioners 1844

Naval veterans were originally housed in the Greenwich Hospital exactly like Chelsea pensioners today. These three pensioners served with Nelson. On the left is Joseph Burgin who lost his leg in the Victory at Trafalgar. He was obviously a favourite with artists, as he appears in a number of paintings and engravings dating from this period

87

'Anchor Type' long service and Good Conduct Medal

This medal was authorised on July 19, 1830 and given to sailors and Royal Marines who were being discharged after 21 years service or more. Gradually the dies used to strike the medal became increasingly worn and cracked. Eventually, in May 1847, this medal — awarded to Colour Sergeant Thomas Chivers RM of HMS Thunderbolt — broke the dies. As a result a new design of medal was introduced

First China War Medal 1843

Issued by the British government for service in the First China War of 1840-42, it was the first official, named campaign medal, produced in the same size and same metal to all ranks for which naval personnel were eligible

The first Naval General Service Medal 1847

This was issued in 1847 with clasps covering 231 actions between 1793 and 1840 and was to survivors only. It had to be claimed. The medal on the left has seven clasps — the most ever placed on one medal. The medal on the right is the only one issued with clasps for all three of Nelson's great victories

The Victoria Cross 1855

The greatest of all British gallantry medals.
Authorised in January 1855, it was issued retrospectively
for acts of gallantry during the Crimean War. This
page from the *Illustrated London News* shows
some of the acts for which the first naval
recipients won their medals

Ordinary Seaman Joseph Trewavas V C

Trewavas won the
Conspicuous Gallantry medal
on July 3, 1855 for cutting adrift
an enemy floating bridge while
under heavy fire. Later he received
the Victoria Cross for the same action.
Note how his medals are pinned
haphazardly to his chest, the usual method
of wearing medals at this time

89

**Presentation of Victoria Crosses for
Japanese War 1865**
Three VCs were won during the Japanese War
at the Battle of Shimonoseki on September 6, 1864.
In accordance with custom, they were presented
at a large parade on Southsea Common. On
the right can be seen the fortifications surrounding
Old Portsmouth

91

Presentation of Victoria Crosses in Hyde Park 1856

The Victoria Cross was always presented with great ceremony
and often by the Queen. The first presentation was a very
grand affair on June 27 at which sixty recipients — including
twelve naval men — received their medals from the Queen

**Stern carvings from HM Yacht
Royal Sovereign**

These carvings are on display in the RN
Museum, Portsmouth

**HM Yacht Royal Sovereign entering
Portsmouth Harbour 1827**

The Royal Sovereign was launched in 1804 and
was the main royal yacht throughout William IV's
reign. Here she is being towed into Portsmouth
Harbour by the early paddle-tug Lightning
after a Fleet Review

Royalty at sea

It was during the nineteenth century that the British Royal Family first became closely associated with the Royal Navy. A spell of active service afloat came to be an indispensable part of the education of all future kings of England

'Royal' Navy

DURING THE NINETEENTH CENTURY, the Royal Family became more involved with the Navy at any time since the Stuarts. Queen Victoria took a lively interest in her fleet and visited squadrons and individual ships constantly during her reign. State visits to British ports and to the continent — always accompanied by naval escorts — became more frequent than before and it was during this period that the custom of marking great national festivals with impressive fleet reviews was fully established. Most important of all, so many members of the Royal Family made their careers in the Navy that a spell of active service afloat seems now to be an indispensible part of the education of all future Kings of England.

This trend was really started by William IV — the 'Sailor King' — who succeeded his elder brother George IV in 1830. He first went to sea at the age of 13 in 1779 and saw action during the closing stages of the War of American Independence — including a full-scale fleet battle with the Spanish off Cape St Vincent in 1780. His father, George III, had insisted that he should be given no special privileges but this rule was waived in 1786 when he was allowed to by-pass the rank of commander and become a full post-Captain in command of the frigate *Pegasus*. He was just twenty. At this time he was serving in the West Indies, where he met Horatio Nelson, then a little-known captain. The two men became close friends, and, in 1787, Prince William gave the bride away when Nelson married Frances Nesbit on the island of Nevis. Nelson had great admiration for the royal sailor and, indeed, he was generally agreed to be an accomplished seaman and a strict but fair

Midshipman Prince William Henry on board HMS Prince George

Second son of George III, joined Navy in 1779 and saw action in War of American Independence. He was not allowed to serve afloat again but continued to rise in rank, becoming Lord High Admiral in 1822

King William IV — The Sailor King

William succeeded his elder brother George IV in 1830 and reigned for seven years. He never lost his bluff sailor's manner and caused amusement in fashionable society by his down-to-earth approach to his new position

93

HRH Prince Alfred

In 1858 Queen Victoria and Prince Albert decided to send their second son Alfred to sea. He made the Navy his career, rising in due course to be Admiral of the Fleet

disciplinarian with officers and men alike.

Unfortunately however, William then spent some years ashore and became associated with his elder brother the Prince of Wales and Charles Fox in their attacks on King George's minister, William Pitt. So, when war again broke out in 1793, Pitt was not prepared to allow the Prince to serve afloat — especially since he was by then Duke of Clarence and a Rear Admiral of the Blue, which might have caused some problems of command. The new Duke sent petitions both to the Admiralty and to his father — but in vain. As the war progressed, he continued to rise slowly up the Navy List but he was never allowed to go on active service. Indeed, the only occasion on which he went to sea again was not until after the war. In 1814, he hoisted his flag — by then, the Union Flag of the Admiral of the Fleet — in the frigate HMS *Janus* to escort the French King Louis XVIII back to his country and, in the same year, he again flew his flag, this time in the battleship *Impregnable*, at a great review held to celebrate — rather prematurely as it turned out! — the defeat of Napoleon. On this occasion, he was heard to direct a volley of choice oaths through his speaking trumpet at an unfortunate sailor who he considered was not 'manning yards' correctly, upon which his brother the Prince Regent, who was standing within earshot, turned to the First Lord of the Admiralty and exclaimed, 'What an excellent officer William is!'

Of course, Napoleon returned from exile and was defeated again at Waterloo but no similar naval celebrations took place on that occasion. William remained ashore but in 1822 he succeeded in reaching the pinnacle of the service when he was created Lord

94

Prince Alfred joins HMS Euryalus

Prince Albert (centre with top hat) is welcomed by Captain Tarleton. Behind him are his two sons, the Prince of Wales (right) and Prince Alfred (left)

HMS Euryalus 1858

Prince Alfred's first ship was this 51-gun
wooden screw frigate. This engraving shows her at
Spithead with Osborne House, the Queen's
summer residence on the left. Under her
bows is the Royal Yacht Elfin

HMS Galatea 1863

Prince Alfred's first command was this 26-gun
screw frigate, launched in 1859. The Prince's
naval career was a normal one except that he was
allowed to by-pass the rank of commander, becoming
a Captain at the very early age of 23

High Admiral — an office which is held nowadays only by the Sovereign. Even in this apparent sinecure he managed to cause trouble and was forced to resign in 1828. Two years later, he became King. He never lost his bluff sailor's manners and, after his accession, he caused much shocked amusement in fashionable society with his very basic language and down-to-earth approach to his new exalted position. But he always remained popular with the Navy and with the people whose imagination was captured by the concept of a Sailor King.

His niece Queen Victoria, who succeeded him in 1837, developed an abiding love for the sea — especially after her marriage to Prince Albert in 1840. Their favourite home was Osborne House on the Isle of Wight, which they first hired in 1844, later buying and completely rebuilding it. To reach Osborne, the Solent had to be crossed and as a result a small fleet of royal yachts came into being. The Queen had inherited the *Royal George*, a lavishly decorated sailing yacht, built in 1817 for George IV while he was still Prince Regent. However, Victoria used the yacht only once, on a visit to Scotland in August 1842, when it had to be towed at a snail's pace of six knots by two small steamers. Apparently, the Queen was so dissatisfied with this slow progress that she made the return journey in a hired paddle-steamer, the *Trident*. Less than eight months later, a new royal yacht was launched. She was called the *Victoria and Albert*, she was powered by steam-driven paddle wheels — and her top speed was 11½ knots!

In all, seven royal yachts were built during the reign and they fell into two distinct categories. There were three larger, sea-going

Visit of Prince Alfred to Australia
The Prince made a world cruise in the Galatea, the highlight of which was a state visit to Australia. Unhappily, the visit was marred by an assassination attempt in which he was severely wounded

The Queen visits HMS Galatea
When the Galatea returned to England, Queen Victoria inspected her as she lay in Osborne Bay. The Queen was in deep mourning as Prince Albert had died only two years before in 1861

THE QUEEN'S YACHTS

Queen Victoria had a small fleet of Royal yachts throughout her reign. Some were large for long sea passages but there were also smaller ones for short voyages, such as the crossing of the Solent to the Queen's summer palace, Osborne House

yachts — all named *Victoria and Albert*. The first, which was superseded in 1855 by a new and larger yacht with more powerful engines, remained in service until 1868 under the name *Osborne*. The new yacht, which was Prince Albert's brain-child and therefore very dear to the Queen, lasted until 1901, when she was finally replaced by a screw-ship of nearly twice her tonnage. All of these yachts were good sea boats and each was a floating palace with full sleeping, living and dining accommodation below decks. They were used on the many royal tours and visits which were such a novel feature of the new reign.

The other four yachts were much smaller. The *Fairy*, an iron screw ship of just over 300 tons launched in 1845, was used for the frequent Solent crossings, since her light draught enabled her to come alongside Trinity Pier, East Cowes to disembark her passengers. She was also used for brief sea excursions by the Royal Family and for shallow-water trips — as in 1848 when the Queen opened the new Steam Basin in Portsmouth Dockyard, and in 1846 when she took the Queen up the Rivers Tamar and Fal during a royal tour of Devon and Cornwall. It was during this particular trip that the young Prince of Wales first appeared in a sailor suit made specially for him by members of the ship's company. It was an immensely popular gesture. The Commander-in-Chief, Portsmouth, signalled 'The Navy is delighted. God Bless our little admiral!' and sailor suits at once became the height of fashion for boys and girls alike. The smallest of all the yachts was the *Elfin* of 98 tons, which first came into commission in 1849. She ran regular trips between Cowes and the mainland while the Queen was in

Queen Victoria in her Coronation Robes

Queen Victoria succeeded her uncle William IV in 1837 and was crowned in Westminster Abbey on June 28, 1838

**Figurehead of
Victoria and Albert II**

The figurehead is on
display in the RN Museum,
Portsmouth

HM Yacht Victoria and Albert I

The first royal steam yacht was launched in
1843. It was renamed Osborne in 1854 and
was broken up in 1868

HM Yacht Royal George c 1890

Queen Victoria inherited the yacht Royal
George, built for George IV in 1817. She used
it very little but it remained in service as
an accommodation ship for the crews of other
royal yachts until 1905

Dining cabin of Victoria and Albert I
Although designed as a sea-going yacht, the first Victoria and Albert was a small and intimate vessel — unlike the floating palaces of later years

residence at Osborne, carrying newspapers, supplies and the all-important despatch boxes. She was known locally as the 'milk boat'. These two yachts, which had only limited accommodation on board, were joined later in the reign by the *Alberta* and the *Osborne II*.

An interesting feature about the earlier yachts was that they were all powered by very modern engines which gave them speeds which were well in excess of many of their contemporaries. In particular, the *Victoria and Albert II* was capable of a top speed of 15 knots at a time when most similarly sized warships could manage only a maximum of between 10 and 12 knots. Their advanced design was due largely to the scientific interests of Prince Albert, and it was indicative of the strikingly modern outlook of the reign. For the first time, the monarch made herself accessible to all her subjects by actually travelling long distances to meet them. The railways and steamships meant that such journeys were both faster and easier than before, but the new trend was due just as much to the influence of both Victoria and Albert themselves who seem to have thoroughly enjoyed travelling. Between 1843 and Albert's death in 1861, there were annual visits to towns and seaports throughout the British Isles, together with a number of state visits to the continent and, for these, the yachts were in constant use. For example, in 1858, the *Victoria and Albert II* took the Princess Royal and her new husband, Prince William Frederick of Prussia, to Antwerp after their wedding, and then went on a cruise to Ferrol and Corunna to test her seagoing capabilities. Later, Prince Albert used her for a visit to Portland, after which the royal

HM Yacht Victoria and Albert II c 1890
This was Queen Victoria's favourite yacht. Launched in 1855 it remained in constant service until 1901

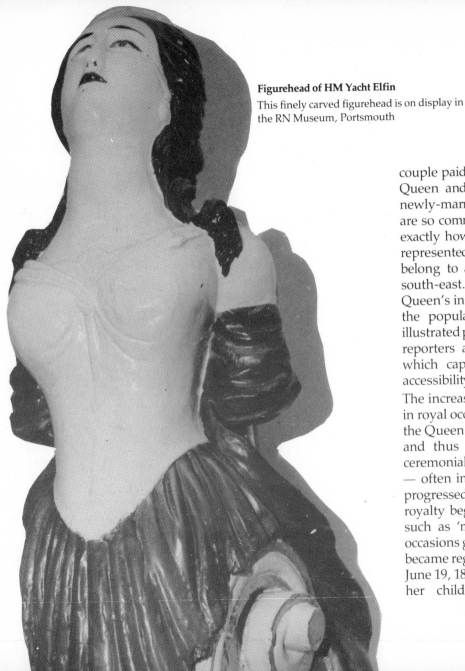

Figurehead of HM Yacht Elfin
This finely carved figurehead is on display in
the RN Museum, Portsmouth

100

couple paid a state visit to Cherbourg in her. Finally, she took the Queen and the Prince to Antwerp on their way to visit their newly-married daughter. Nowadays, when world tours by royalty are so common as to be unremarkable, it is difficult to appreciate exactly how great a revolution this dramatic increase in mobility represented. For the first time the British royal family was seen to belong to all their people and not just to the capital and the south-east. This new approach — as striking in its way as our own Queen's introduction of 'walkabouts' — led to a significant rise in the popularity of the monarchy which was reflected in the illustrated papers. Wherever the Queen went, she was followed by reporters and artists and some charming engravings resulted which capture much of the excitement caused by this new accessibility.

The increase in royal visits meant that the Navy became involved in royal occasions to a much greater extent than before. Wherever the Queen went, she had to be escorted and guarded by warships and thus naval personnel were increasingly acquainted with ceremonial and etiquette. Monarchs had visited their fleets before — often in state — but never so frequently and so, as the reign progressed, standard procedures for receiving and acknowledging royalty began to evolve. At first, only long-established customs such as 'manning the yards' were followed but gradually the occasions grew in size and complexity, until full-scale fleet reviews became regular occasions. There was a minor review at Spithead in June 19, 1845, when the Queen, accompanied by Prince Albert and her children, inspected the Experimental Squadron. This

HM Yacht Fairy in Portsmouth Dockyard 1848

This iron, screw yacht was launched in 1845. She was 300 tons and was used for brief sea voyages and shallow-water trips

HM Yacht Elfin leaving Portsmouth Harbour c 1890

The Elfin was known as the 'milk boat' because she ran regular trips between Cowes and the mainland while the Queen was in residence at Osborne House

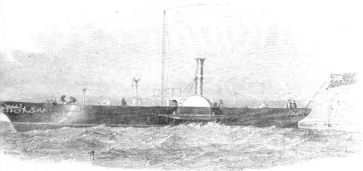

HM Yacht Elfin 1849

The smallest of all the royal yachts was designed especially for the Solent crossing

The Royal yachts

A composite painting showing the Royal yacht fleet c 1860. (Left to right) HMY Royal George, Elfin, Victoria and Albert II and Osborne (ex Victoria and Albert I). Below is the earliest photograph of royal yachts in the RN Museum's collection. (Left to right): Victoria and Albert II, Osborne II (L 1870) and Royal George

State visit to Scotland 1842

The Royal George was towed to Scotland by two small steam tugs. The Queen was so dissatisfied with the slow speed that she made the return journey in a hired paddle-steamer

State visits and royal occasions

Railways and steamships made travelling much easier and so Queen Victoria and her family were seen by more of her subjects than any of her predecessors. This new mobility was as important in those days as the innovation of our own Queen's 'walkabouts'

consisted of eight sailing battleships which had been assembled specially to test the qualities of different designs of ship. On August 11 1853, there was a much grander affair when, for the first time, a fleet of steamships was assembled for royal inspection. Six steam battleships and 16 smaller vessels performed various evolutions, including a sham attack on a fleet of sailing ships and a race between the steamers. The review aroused so much public interest that Portsmouth was jammed with crowds on the night before and many visitors went without beds.

Less than a year later, on March 11 1854, the spectacle was repeated, but this time in earnest. War with Russia was imminent and the government had decided to send a hurriedly-raised squadron to the Baltic to blockade the enemy fleet and to disrupt trade. Eleven battleships and 10 smaller ships — each one powered by steam — were assembled under the command of Vice-Admiral Sir Charles Napier for inspection by the Queen. Her Majesty received all the senior officers of the fleet on board the *Fairy* and then led the ships on the first stage of their journey as far as the Nab. A few days later, she once more ventured out to Spithead to witness the departure of the second division of the Baltic Fleet and, once again, she led the ships to sea in the *Fairy*, although this time it was noted that the Queen seemed reluctant to part company and, despite a strong wind and rough seas, stayed with the fleet for much longer than planned. Indeed, as a number of observers commented, the mood of this warlike review differed greatly from that of its predecessor. The *Illustrated London News* pointed out that there was no dressing of ships and manning of yards and

Embarkation of the Queen at Woolwich

These woodcuts are taken from the first volume of the *Illustrated London News*, which was published on May 14, 1842

concluded:

'. . . The naval review of last summer was a great national holiday, with people in their holiday clothes and the ships in their holiday colours . . . But Saturday's proceedings had no holiday air about them . . . the people who came in their thousands from all parts of the country to see the fleet off wore an earnest and thoughtful expression of countenance and seemed fully alive to the importance of the coming struggle . . .'

However, all these previous displays paled into insignificance when compared with the massive review held on April 23 1856, to celebrate the signing of the peace treaty. A fleet of nearly 250 ships — 22 steam battleships, 16 steam frigates and sloops and numerous gunboats and armoured batteries — was assembled at Spithead and inspected by the Queen. It was on this occasion that the ceremonial first began to take the elaborate form which is still very largely followed today. The Royal Yacht — the brand-new *Victoria and Albert II* — emerged from Portsmouth Harbour to the acompaniment of thunderous gun salutes from the waiting fleet and then proceeded to steam slowly through the lines. As she did so, the ships' crews manned the yards and cheered. Arriving at the head of the lines, the Royal Yacht anchored and the senior officers of the fleet then went on board to be presented to the Queen. Finally, the whole fleet weighed anchor and was led to sea by the *Victoria and Albert* as far as the Nab. Here, the yacht took up a position close to two pivot ships, round which the great battleships and their consorts steamed majestically, their crews manning the rigging and cheering as they did so. The day ended with a sham

Visit of the King of France to Britain 1844

King Louis Phillippe arrived in Portsmouth Harbour in the steamer Gomer on October 8. (above) He was then taken by boat to the Royal Clarence Yard, where he boarded a special train for Windsor (opposite page)

Opening of the new steam basin Portsmouth Dockyard 1848

Queen Victoria set the pattern for modern royal duties. Here, accompanied by Prince Albert, she opens the new steam basin at Portsmouth

gunboat attack on Southsea Castle and a grand firework display, at the conclusion of which the fleet was brightly illuminated. This tremendous exhibition of seapower proved immensely popular and was watched by a crowd of 600,000. The *Illustrated London News* commented:

'. . . Never at any period in our history have we been able, even at the outbreak of a war, to boast of a fleet as powerful in numbers and weight of metal as that which floats at Spithead. Such a mighty gathering of First Rates and gunboats may not for years again be witnessed in these waters . . .'

The prediction was proved right. The public found the next review, of 1867, a disappointing affair since, by then, the towering wooden battleships were fast being replaced by the squat black ironclads and the size of the fleet was much reduced while the revolutionary new ships were being brought into service. It was not until 1887 and 1897 that similar spectacles were seen at Spithead and then the fleets which were assembled overshadowed even the 1856 review.

The close association of this kind of impressive royal ceremonial with the Navy served greatly to increase the popularity of the service, which had been in the limelight very little since 1815. Reviews provided an excellent opportunity for the ordinary people to see their fleet in the most dramatic manner possible and Spithead was a perfect amphitheatre. The water was deep and broad enough to accommodate the very largest ships, while the cliffs of Ryde and the sands of Stokes Bay and Southsea provided many excellent vantage points. So popular were the displays of

1854 and 1856, that formal fleet reviews soon became a permanent feature of every important state occasion — from declarations of war, to visits by foreign heads of state. These magnificent spectacles were yet another expression of the growing links between the monarchy and the Navy.

However, the most significant indication of those links came in 1858, when Queen Victoria and Prince Albert decided to send their second son, Alfred, to sea. Like his great-uncle William IV Alfred started young, as a cadet in the steam frigate *Euryalus*. But, unlike his predecessor, his naval career was virtually uninterrupted — apart from occasional periods of extra leave to enable him to carry out his royal duties. He had a most successful period of training as midshipman and lieutenant during which he demonstrated that, unlike his brother, the Prince of Wales, he had inherited his father's keen brain and flair for mathematics. He was allowed to by-pass the rank of commander in the same way as his great-uncle and so became captain of HMS *Galatea*, a steam frigate, in 1867 when he was just 23 — extremely young indeed for that period! In the *Galatea*, he made a world tour — narrowly escaping assassination in Sydney, Australia on the way, and then went on to command two first-class ironclads in the Mediterranean, HMS *Sultan* and *Black Prince*. He was promoted to Rear-Admiral in 1878 and commanded successively the Naval Reserves, the Channel Squadron, the Mediterranean Fleet and at Plymouth, until finally, in 1893, he succeeded his uncle as Duke of Saxe-Coburg and so had to resign from the Navy, retaining only the honorary rank of Admiral of the Fleet. But his career — apart from the slight

State visit to Scotland 1848

The Queen and her family are welcomed aboard
the Royal Yacht by Captain Fitzclarence, a
natural son of William IV

'acceleration' at commander level! — had been similar in every way
to those of other leading Victorian admirals.

The success of Prince Alfred's career established an important
precedent and the Prince of Wales sent both his sons to sea for a
time and the younger son, George, made the Navy his career. In
due course, he too decided on a naval education for *his* second son
and, by a strange coincidence, both of them unexpectedly became
King — as George V and George VI. Alfred's influence was also felt
in another more distant branch of the family. Between 1863 and
1866, he paid a number of visits to his sister Alice who had married
the Grand Duke of Hesse, and during these visits he met the
young Prince Louis of Battenburg, who was so inspired by the
splendid young lieutenant and his rousing stories of adventure at
sea that he determined to be a sailor himself. Nothing less than the
Royal Navy would do so, in 1868, he became a naturalised
Englishman and began a distinguished career, eventually
becoming First Sea Lord in 1912. He too was followed by his sons,
the younger of whom was Lord Louis Mountbatten and he, in his
turn, later encouraged his nephew Prince Philip to join the Navy.
So the present Royal Family's very close ties with the Senior
Service can really be traced back to 1858 — when Queen Victoria
and Prince Albert made their decision about the future of young
Prince Alfred.

State visit to Scotland 1848

The royal yacht (Victoria and Albert I)
leaving Woolwich

**State visit to
Ireland 1849**

The Queen going on board the
royal yacht Victoria and Albert I
in Osborne Bay prior to leaving
for Ireland

State visit to Ireland 1849

Queen Victoria and Prince Albert waving to the crowds in Kingstown Harbour

State visit to France 1858

The royal yacht Victoria and Albert II entering Cherbourg Harbour

Royal Summer visit to Cornwall 1846
The Victoria and Albert I (right) and Fairy (left) are seen in Mounts Bay

Royal Summer visit to Cornwall 1846

The Fairy in the River Fal

The Queen's Annual Cruise 1852
Before the death of Prince Albert in 1861, the Queen and her family regularly went on a summer cruise to various ports in Britain

Arrival of the Prince of Wales in Canada 1860
As the royal children grew up, they began to
undertake state duties of their own. Here, the Prince
of Wales arrives in Halifax to begin a visit to Canada.
He made the voyage in the battleship HMS Hero
(left background)

114

**Departure of Prince and Princess Frederick William of Prussia
February 1858**
Queen Victoria's eldest daughter married the Crown Prince of Prussia in
1858 and the new royal yacht was used to ferry the newly married couple
across the Channel

The marriage of the Prince of Wales 1863
The royal yacht with the bride on board,
arrives at the Nore. Astern of her, in the centre,
is her predecessor, now renamed the Osborne

The marriage of the Prince of Wales 1863

The Victoria and Albert II, with the bride Princess
Alexandra on board, arrives at Flushing on her way
to England. She is being saluted by two of the new
ironclads, HMS Defence (centre) and Resistance (right)

117

Fleet reviews

The increasing number of visits by sea meant that the Navy became more involved in royal occasions. Gradually, the ceremonial became more complex and eventually full-scale fleet reviews became a regular feature of every important state or royal event

Review of the special steam squadron 1853

This was the first occasion on which a steam squadron of any size had been on show, and after the Queen's inspection the ships were led out to sea where they performed fleet evolutions — including a sham attack on a squadron of sailing ships

Review of the special steam squadron 1853

Six steam battleships and sixteen smaller vessels assembled at Spithead for inspection by the Queen. Here she and her family are being rowed to the flagship HMS Duke of Wellington

Review of the battle fleet 1854

At the outbreak of the Crimean War, the Queen inspected the Baltic Fleet before it sailed to its war station. This title page to a special supplement to the *Illustrated London News* shows the flagship HMS Duke of Wellington

THE BALTIC FLEET

ILLUSTRATED LONDON NEWS SUPPLEMENT

MARCH 18, 1854

Review of the Baltic Fleet 1854

The Queen in HM yacht Fairy, led the fleet on the short first leg of its voyage. Here the Fairy is shown in the centre dwarfed by the steam corvette Tribune (left) and the steam battleship St Jean D'Acre (right)

119

Review of the Baltic Fleet 1854

The Queen receives the Commander-in-Chief, Admiral Sir Charles Napier, on board the royal yacht Fairy

The Peace Review 1856

All previous reviews were dwarfed by the massive review, held to celebrate peace on April 23, 1856. A fleet of nearly 250 ships was assembled at Spithead for inspection by the Queen and the climax came when all the ships present steamed past the royal yacht with their crews manning the rigging

The Peace Review 1856

More than 600,000 people watched the review from the shores of Portsmouth, Gosport and the Isle of Wight. Here the holiday crowd streams off the Floating Bridge that crossed Portsmouth Harbour

Nowhere to stay

So many people came to
Portsmouth for the peace review
that many had nowhere to stay.
This caricature by 'Phiz' shows
the plight of some of the
unfortunate spectators

Fleet Review Ceremonial — Manning the rigging

One of the most spectacular
features of the Victorian fleet
reviews was the sight of
hundreds of sailors standing
upright on the ships'
yards. Here, under orders
from the boatswain, the
sailors rush into the rigging

THE GRAND NAVAL REVIEW.

SUPPLEMENT TO THE ILLUSTRATED LONDON NEWS

**Fleet Review ceremonial
— Manning the yards**

The final effect of the ceremony of manning the
rigging takes place. Arranging the many flags in the
manner shown on the right is called 'Dressing
overall', a custom that is still followed on
special occasions today

122

Fleet Review ceremonial — The Ball
The wide, open upper decks of the old wooden battleships and early ironclads provided ideal areas for dancing

Policemen of the world

During most of the nineteenth century, the Royal
Navy acted as a universal peacekeeping force. Slavery
and piracy were stamped out and tension relieved in all
corners of the globe by the constant vigilance of the
British men of war

Seapower in action

To most Britons, the word SEAPOWER is immensely evocative, conjuring up visions of long lines of stately sailing battleships or looming grey dreadnoughts locked in mortal combat amidst the thunder of heavy guns and the swirl of acrid smoke. But such images are over-simplified. In the first place, it is perfectly possible for a country to gain command of the seas without actually fighting for it. In 1805 Napoleon's plans for an invasion of England, supported by his fleets, were checked when the British concentrated a large naval force in the Western Approaches. The French realised that they could not seize command of the Channel without a battle in which their losses would be unacceptably high and so decided to abandon the operation. Strictly speaking, therefore, Trafalgar did not 'save England from invasion': the truly decisive moment had occurred months before. Again, during the Victorian period the Royal Navy did not fight a single fleet action and British battleships fired their guns in anger on only six major occasions — each time against shore batteries. And yet, as we shall see, seapower was as potent a force then as in the years 1793 - 1815.

Secondly, once command of the seas has been gained, either by a battle or by more passive means, it still has to be seen to be used or else it is meaningless. Capital ships may appear to be the embodiment of seapower because they look so impressive, but it is the smaller ships of the fleet which in fact put that power into practice. During the Great War of 1793 - 1815 the battlefleets were like an umbrella beneath the shelter of which the frigates and other 'cruisers' patrolled the trade routes, protected convoys and attacked enemy colonies. Exactly the same pattern was followed in peacetime. The much depleted battlefleets remained concentrated close to home, keeping potential rivals in check, while the smaller vessels were dispersed in scattered squadrons, taking Britain's influence to all corners of the globe. Indeed, as Britain's worldwide interests increased, so the ships became more and more dispersed, although the actual number in commission remained much the same. In 1830, 101 out of the 160 vessels in full commission were concentrated close to home. The other 59 were serving in the East and West Indies, off Africa and in South America. By 1870, there were 180 ships in commission but only 86 — just under half — were in European waters. The East Indies squadron had grown to 31 — four times its 1830 size — and there were new squadrons in the Pacific and off Australia, as well as a specially formed 'Flying Squadron' which was undertaking a world cruise. ' . . . It is fortunate,' wrote a despairing First Lord of the Admiralty, 'that the world is not larger, for there is no other limit to the service of the fleet . . . '

The tasks performed by these widely scattered ships were many and varied. Perhaps the most arduous — and certainly the most dangerous — was the suppression of slavery and of piracy. Piracy was rife all over the world during the nineteenth century and so the fight against it was always spasmodic. There were small, single-ship actions such as the rescue by HMS *Polyphemus* of an English brig captured by Moorish pirates in 1848. And there were full-scale, organised campaigns such as those mounted by 'Rajah' Brooke. Brooke was a typical example of an enthusiastic Victorian

Attack on Borneo pirates 1845
Some of the most vicious pirates in eastern waters were subdued in a series of campaigns, mostly inspired and led by 'Rajah' Brooke

The fight against slavery
The capture of a slaver by HM Brig Arab in 1856

colonial administrator. Extrovert, charismatic and inspired with a strong religious fervour, he devoted his life to the extermination of piracy in Borneo and to the 'civilising' of that savage land. In 1843, he persuaded Captain Henry Keppel of HMS *Dido* to take part in a river-borne attack on two of the chief pirate strongholds. A similar campaign was mounted the following year, again with the assistance of the *Dido* and of an East India Company steamer, the *Phlegethon*. By 1845, the Commander-in-Chief East Indies had become involved in Brooke's crusade and even bigger campaigns ensued until, in 1849, a large pirate fleet was intercepted by a British flotilla and over 70 *prahus* (pirate vessels) destroyed or driven ashore. Thereafter, the Borneo pirates gave much less trouble.

All these campaigns were conducted entirely on the initiative of the men on the spot, but the fight against slavery was more closely controlled by the Admiralty and was carried out in accordance with the official policy of successive British governments. Britain had abolished the slave trade in 1807 and, in 1838, outlawed slavery altogether in her dominions. However, this by no means ended the trade, since other countries continued to base their economies on slave labour and there were numerous unscrupulous ship-owners of all nationalities who were eager to make an easy profit by transporting negroes from West Africa to Brazil, Cuba or the southern states of the USA. So, in an attempt to stamp out the evil, the British government stationed ships off the west coast of Africa and in the West Indies with orders to capture any ship suspected of carrying slaves. It was a thankless task,

HMS Brisk's prize
The slaver Sunny South is apprehended by
HMS Brisk in 1860

127

HMS Maeander at Rio de Janeiro 1851

Between 1848 and 1851, HMS Maeander was sent
on a flag-showing cruise under Captain Henry
Keppel. This took her right round the world

involving weeks of endless beating up and down on the known slave routes, with only the excitement of an occasional chase to relieve the monotony. Moreover, there were international complications. Freedom of search on the high seas was a jealously guarded right and very few countries were prepared to allow Britain a completely free hand. In particular, the United States, who had gone to war with Britain in 1812 over this very issue, refused to allow the Royal Navy to search any suspect vessels which were flying the American flag — although they did maintain a small anti-slavery squadron to deal with their own offenders. Not surprisingly, nearly every slaver carried a Stars and Stripes in its flag locker and many guilty ships were able to escape scot-free. Above all, the death-rate in the African squadron was the highest in the Navy because of the dangers of yellow fever and malaria. Between 1825 and 1842, 54 men out of every 1000 on the African station died while on active service. During the same period, nine men out of 1000 died in the Home Fleet and 15 out of 1000 in the East Indies Squadron.

If the fight cost many lives, it was also expensive in *materiel*. Slaving ships were built for speed and manoeuvrability and they had to be caught with the evidence actually in them if they were to be legally detained. So, in order to do the work of prevention efficiently, large numbers of warships were needed. In 1830, the Cape and West Africa squadrons together had 11 ships. By 1840, the number had risen to 34 and even at the height of the Crimean War in 1855, there were 22 ships in African waters. All slavers caught red-handed were taken to Freetown where the slaves were freed (hence its name); the captured ships valued by a special Admiralty court and prize money (known as 'head' money) was assessed on behalf of the captors. Often, these rewards were quite generous which gave a slightly mercenary edge to the philanthropic endeavours of the anti-slavery squadron! All the same, thanks to the efforts of these ships, and to the anti-slavery crusade of President Abraham Lincoln of the United States, the Atlantic slave trade had dwindled to nothing by the early 1860s and, after 1865, the centre of attention was transferred to East Africa where an equally vicious trade existed with Arabia and Madagascar.

In addition to these costly campaigns, the Navy also performed other equally altruistic but less dangerous tasks. The electric telegraph was developed in the 1840s and was soon spreading all over the globe. The most important link-up was the transatlantic cable between Newfoundland and Ireland and, appropriately, Royal Naval ships were involved in its laying. The preliminary survey of the route was performed in 1857 by the paddle sloop *Cyclops*, and in August of that year the screw battleship *Agamemnon*, accompanied by the US screw frigate *Niagara*, began laying the cable. After 335 miles had been laid, it parted but the next year another attempt was made by the same ships and this proved successful. Unfortunately, the cable worked for only a short time and it was not until 1866 that a permanent telegraphic link was established.

Channel Squadron at Cork 1853

At a time when Ireland was in constant ferment, the battleships of the Channel Squadron paid regular visits to the south coast of the troubled province

British Squadron in the Bay of Naples 1860

The British remained neutral during the Italian crisis of 1860, but ships of the Mediterranean fleet maintained a watchful presence

One of the main reasons why naval personnel and ships were used in this venture was that the Royal Navy led the world in oceanic surveying. A Hydrographic Department had been established at the Admiralty as early as 1795 and, after the conclusion of the war, it had grown rapidly, thanks mainly to the leadership of Sir Francis Beaufort, the man who devised the Beaufort Wind Scale. Marine surveys were carried out all over the world, providing accurate information that still forms the basis of the internationally respected Admiralty charts. For example, the voyage of HMS *Beagle* in 1831, which was made famous by the presence of the naturalist and philosopher Charles Darwin, was primarily a surveying exercise and Darwin's great discoveries were purely incidental. Under the direction of Commander Robert Fitzroy, one of the most gifted hydrographers in the Navy at that time, the *Beagle* made a meticulous survey of the Straits of Magellan and of some of the Pacific Islands. Similar surveys were also made by other hydrographers of the east and west coasts of Africa, of Borneo and the East Indies and of the Great Barrier Reef off Australia. Additionally, ships of the Indian Navy surveyed the Red Sea, the Persian Gulf and Burma. In all, it was vital work which benefitted not only Britain, but the whole world.

However, probably the Navy's greatest contribution to scientific knowledge was in the field of exploration. Most of the great voyages of discovery in the Victorian period were made by naval personnel in naval ships, following the example of their illustrious predecessors Cook and Vancouver. The first important voyages were made by Captain William Parry who tried unsuccessfully to find the North West Passage around North America. Although his voyages failed in their main aim, they nevertheless contributed much to the knowledge of polar regions, since his ships deliberately wintered in the area and, as a result, many valuable lessons were learned about survival in such difficult conditions. In particular, canned meat was first tried out during these voyages and proved a most successful way of preserving food. The meat was compressed into tins which were then boiled until the air inside had been driven out. The French name for the resulting meat was *boeuf bouilli* (boiled beef) and this gave rise to the famous nickname: 'bully beef.'

Parry was followed to the Arctic by James Ross, who also pioneered Antarctic exploration, and by the most famous Arctic explorer of all — Captain Sir John Franklin. Franklin made a number of successful voyages but, ironically, he is remembered best because, in 1845, he led an expedition which ended in disaster. His ships, the *Erebus* and *Terror* were trapped in the ice for two successive winters; Franklin himself died in June 1847 and the survivors, unable to endure a third winter in the ice with insufficient and unwholesome food, abandoned their ships and tried to reach safety in boats and sledges. All of them died. Meanwhile, in England, concern grew and search parties were sent out. For 10 years, the first aim of all Arctic expeditions was to find Franklin. And then, in 1859, a party under Commander Francis McClintock, himself an experienced Arctic explorer, found the pathetic remains of the last survivors at Point Victoria on King William Island. It was a national disaster, but it was felt particularly

131

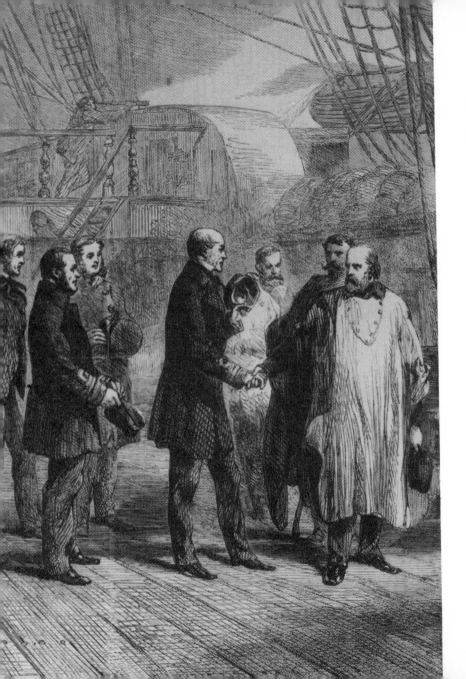

Garibaldi's farewell to Rear-Admiral Mundy
The liberator of Italy visits the C-in-C of the British
squadron and thanks him for his friendly 'neutrality' which
had contributed greatly to his success

keenly by the Navy, since Franklin's great reputation had
encouraged many promising young officers to volunteer to join
him and their deaths were a grave loss to the service. Following
McClintock's return with his sad news, there was a lull in polar
exploration and it was not until 1875 that British naval explorers
ventured into the Arctic again.

Another task which the Navy undertook in this period was
'showing the flag'. Disturbances in Ireland in 1848 and again in
1853, were countered by sending the Channel Fleet to Cork
Harbour to make a discreet show of strength. The various scattered
squadrons were encouraged to make regular visits to friendly ports
and, occasionally, individual ships were sent on special cruises.
For example, between February 1848 and July 1851, Captain Henry
Keppel took the sailing frigate *Maeander* around the world, visiting
Singapore, Borneo, Hong Kong, Australia, Tahiti and South
America en route. In 1870, the practice was regularised by the
formation of a special 'Flying Squadron' which was sent on a
world-wide deployment lasting two years.

One of the most striking demonstrations of how seapower could
be used in a non-aggressive way to make a diplomatic point, came
in 1860 during the Italian crisis. At that time, Italy comprised a
squabbling group of separate states and one man, Giuseppe
Garibaldi, set himself finally to solve the problem. He resolved to
take control of the Island of Sicily — then part of the Kingdom of
Naples — with the help of a small band of followers known as 'The
Thousand', intending to use the island as a base from which he
could mount a full-scale invasion of the mainland of Italy.

Although there was much public support in Britain for Garibaldi — a privately raised 'English Regiment' actually fought in his army — the official British policy was one of neutrality. Nonetheless, a detachment of the Mediterranean fleet under Rear-Admiral Sir Rodney Mundy was sent to patrol the northern coast of Sicily and, on May 11, these ships interposed themselves between a Neapolitan squadron and two transports bearing Garibaldi's tiny invasion force. As a result, the *Garibaldani* landed unopposed in Sicily at Marsala and began a successful campaign. By mid-June the whole island was in the hands of the insurgents and, on August 18, Garibaldi crossed the Straits of Messina, closely watched but unmolested by the British fleet, and began his conquest of the Italian mainland.

Eventually, King Victor Emmanuel of Piedmont was proclaimed the First King of Italy and Garibaldi, having achieved his aim, relinquished his power and returned to his island home of Caprera. But his last act before leaving was symbolic: he visited Admiral Mundy on board his flagship HMS *Hannibal* and thanked him for his support! Technically the Royal Navy had done nothing but in fact Admiral Mundy's 'neutrality' had been exercised in Garibaldi's favour. The British squadron had been in a position to stop the rebellion at the outset by preventing 'The Thousand' from reaching Sicily; instead, in a quiet and unobtrusive way, the British had been able to show their sympathy for Garibaldi without actually intervening forcibly — a task for which warships were — and still are! — admirably suited. As Lord Palmerston wrote to Admiral Napier in 1847 '. . . There are no better peacekeepers than

well-appointed three-deckers . . .'

Despite these many peaceful tasks, the Navy still remained ready for war. Although the period has become known as the Age of the Pax Britannica, there was in fact scarcely a year between 1830 and 1870 when sailors were not engaged in fighting somewhere in the world. Britain had emerged from the Great War with many overseas territories which required constant policing and consolidation. And 'consolidation' almost invariably entailed the conquest and annexation of neighbouring countries in a ceaseless attempt to render the vast, scattered and unwieldy mass of colonies secure. Clearly, it was impossible for a country the size of Britain to maintain large garrisons in all her possessions. Instead, at the first sign of rebellion, ships were diverted from the scattered squadrons to the trouble-spots — a move which could be made with far greater ease than the laborious transportation of a special army. Thus, it was seapower which held the British Empire together.

Indeed, trouble often could be settled by the application of naval force alone. In 1840 Mehemet Ali, the ruler of Egypt under the Sultan of Turkey, revolted against his overlord and invaded Syria. Britain, France and Austria decided to intervene on the side of Turkey and so the Mediterranean fleet, together with some Austrian and Turkish ships, was sent to the Middle East to assist the Turkish forces. Mehemet Ali's son, Ibrahim Pasha, with an army of more than 70,000, was sweeping all before him as he pushed northwards but the arrival of the allied fleet dramatically reversed the situation. The Egyptian fleet was blockaded in

Alexandria, thus effectively cutting off Ibrahim's sea-borne supplies and reinforcements and, at the same time, a series of attacks were mounted on Egyptian-held ports in Syria. The British, in particular, under the vigorous leadership of Commodore Charles Napier, took part in a number of amphibious operations, including the capture of Sidon. Eventually, on November 3, a powerful detachment of the allied fleet mounted a naval attack on the key town of Acre and, after a fierce battle in which the new methods of gunnery training taught at HMS *Excellent* amply proved themselves, the main Egyptian magazine was blown up and the fortifications were demolished. Ibrahim's forces abandoned the town and began to retreat southwards. On November 27, a peace treaty was signed and the threat from Egypt

was over. Hardly any troops at all had been involved: bombardments and naval landing parties had been sufficient.

A similar pattern was followed in the Anglo-Japanese War of 1863-1864. This was a classic case of a clash of two nations with widely different cultures; each of which considered the other barbarians. Britain and other western countries wished to trade with Japan: the *Shogun* (Chief Minister), who was anxious to allow westerners into the country, was opposed for mainly political reasons by the powerful *Daimios* (feudal princes), who preferred to maintain Japan's traditional isolation from outside influences. In 1862, a British merchant was murdered in a street brawl by a retainer of the Daimio of Satsuma who, not unnaturally, refused to make any reparation or to deliver up the culprit to justice. Britain's

Altruistic tasks

Besides keeping the peace, the Royal Navy also undertook many other non-aggressive missions which benefitted not just Britain but the whole world

reply was automatic. Ships were detached from the East Indies squadron under the command of Vice Admiral Augustus Kuper and, on August 15 1863, Satsuma's capital of Kagoshima was bombarded and set on fire. However, the British ships were badly mauled by their opponents who proved to be far better gunners than had been expected. Accordingly, the Japanese opposition to the hated foreigners was only strengthened and other Daimios joined Satsuma in his stand. Kuper called in reinforcements and conferred with his European naval colleagues and eventually, on September 1864, a combined British, French and Dutch squadron bombarded and silenced a powerful series of forts at Shimonoseki, the stronghold of the Daimio of Nagato. The following day, landing parties were put ashore to spike the guns and destroy the forts, upon which Nagato decided to make peace. Satsuma also gave way and the westerners were allowed to continue their trading — thanks, once again, to the long arm of seapower.

That long arm could also reach far inland if there was a navigable river available. Key enemy towns could be bombarded and expeditionary forces with full equipment transported swiftly, using small ships. In Burma, where there were hardly any roads at all, so that rivers were almost the only means of communication, naval forces were absolutely vital to the success of the two wars of 1824 - 26 and 1850 - 53. As we have seen, the gunboats which were built too late for the Crimean War were not wasted, since they were sent on the long sea-voyage to the Far East, where they rendered sterling service on the rivers during the Second China War of 1857-60. And in the First China War of 1840-42, it was a small ship,

The Transatlantic Telegraph Cable 1858

HMS Agamemnon (left) and USS Niagara (right) take aboard cable at Keyham. The 91-gun screw battleship HMS Agamemnon (below), was launched in 1852 and was converted temporarily in 1858 for cable-laying

The Flying Squadron at Plymouth 1870

This specially formed squadron undertook a two-year worldwide deployment — mainly to show the flag

135

Stern of USS Niagara
The 40-gun screw frigate which laid the American half of the cable

the Honourable East India Company Steamer *Nemesis,* which captured most of the lime-light. She was an iron-built, flat bottomed paddlesteamer of 660 tons, drawing only five feet of water and armed with two 32 pounder guns. She was ideal for river work and took part in 24 different engagements during the war, including the bombardment of Canton and the capture of Shanghai. On one occasion, she is reputed to have sunk 11 junks before breakfast! Her commander, William Hutcheson Hall, began the war only as a Master's Mate, which is roughly equivalent to a modern sub-lieutenant, even though he had been on active service for more than 28 years. However, the gallant exploits of his tiny ship won him accelerated promotion to Lieutenant in 1841, Commander in 1843 and Captain in 1844. His crew obviously enjoyed the dashing brand of hit and run warfare in which Hall excelled, since they presented him with a specially-inscribed sword 'as a tribute of respect.' And Hall himself behaved in exactly the same way during the Baltic campaign of 1854, while commanding the much larger paddle sloop *Hecla,* although on that occasion he was reprimanded for over eagerness!

Indeed, eagerness, dash and simple courage characterised the Navy's general approach to river warfare — although that courage was occasionally indistinguishable from foolhardiness. There was a strong naval tradition for such an attitude since many of the most gallant — and the most bloody — actions of the Great War had been fought in open ships' boats. Enemy ships had been 'cut out' of heavily defended harbours and shore installations such as semaphore stations and forts had been destroyed. In 1810, the

Marine surveying — the voyage of the Beagle
The Beagle, seen here beached in the River Santa Cruz for repairs, made a number of surveying voyages. The most famous was in 1831-34 under Commander Robert Fitzroy when Charles Darwin sailed in her as the expedition's naturalist

Admiralty had become so concerned by the high casualties in these operations, that they had issued a General Order stating that, despite the admiration they felt for such 'brilliant achievements', they were nevertheless of the opinion that 'this kind of warfare has been carried too far' and, accordingly, they ordered that such actions should not be undertaken 'when the object to be gained is not of sufficient importance to justify the risk of lives'. Nonetheless, the actions had continued and, when the Naval General Service Medal was instituted, their importance was acknowledged by the authorisation of 56 special clasps for particularly notable 'boat services'.

Actions of this type continued throughout the Victorian period. A classic example occurred during the Second China War and again involved Henry Keppel. In the summer of 1857, the British made a major push up of the Canton River with the intention of capturing the important provincial capital of Canton. A small fleet of gunboats, brigs and corvettes under Commodore Keppel's command reached Fatsham Creek on May 30, where they encountered a strong force of Imperial junks moored in two mutually supporting lines. On June 1, the British attacked. First into action were the gunboats, but they soon grounded in the shallows, whereupon the ships' boats, with Keppel at their head in his galley, stormed the first line of junks and captured them. However, they now came under a withering fire from the second Chinese line and a number of boats were sunk, including Keppel's own galley. Keppel therefore ordered his forces to retire on the gunboats which had managed to edge closer on the rising tide.

Almost as soon as the exhausted men had reached the shelter of the gunboats, Keppel was preparing a fresh attack. According to his own account, he cried 'Let us try the row boats once more boys', although Midshipman Victor Montagu, who was standing close by, thought that he put it a little more forcibly; 'The beggars are making off! Man the boats. You rascals!' (shaking his fist at the Chinese) 'I'll pay you off for this!' Whatever it was he said, it had an instant effect.

'...At that moment,' wrote Keppel, 'there arose from the boats, as if every man took it up at the same instant, one of those British cheers so full of meaning that I knew at once it was all up with John Chinaman...'

Midshipman Montagu, who had been ordered to remain in the gunboat, saw the attack from a distance:

'...What a rush! Fresh boats had come up; a frantic cheer was given; and on they raced exactly like boats at a regatta, indiscriminately, straight at the junks, which now appeared to be getting into position with their oars to make away..'

They were indeed retreating but they could not escape. For seven miles they were harried by the little boats until finally all but three had been captured or driven ashore. Reading about the battle in cold blood, it sounds as if Keppel took an inexcusable risk but, in fact, he lost only 80 men killed and wounded out of a total force of 1900. A glorious action indeed— and but one of many in which the Navy demonstrated that, whatever changes it was undergoing, it had lost none of its almost boyish offensive spirit.

All the same, it was not the Victorian sailor's undoubted courage which captured the public imagination, so much as his adaptability. We have already seen some of the tasks to which he put his hand but none of these attracted so much attention as when he turned soldier. Amphibious warfare was not new to the Navy. Sailors and Royal Marines had landed frequently during the wars of the eighteenth century to assist in sieges of key enemy coastal towns and, during the Great War, they had been active ashore in the capture of most of the important French and Dutch Colonies such as Martinique and Java. But, normally, these had been only brief interludes, and in any case their work in these distant lands had been overshadowed by the succession of great naval victories at sea. During the minor wars of the nineteenth century, there were no such distractions. When the troubles broke out and warships were diverted to the beleaguered colonies, they usually found the local forces completely outnumbered and so parties of Royal Marines, their ranks invariably swelled by bluejackets, were landed to assist. Moreover, thanks to the training of HMS *Excellent,* the seamen were expert artillerymen and their guns nearly always had greater ranges than the lighter army field pieces. As a result the 'Naval Brigades', as these bodies of seamen were called, became a familiar feature of almost every colonial war and the average bluejacket saw more action on land alongside the redcoats than he did at sea in his ships.

One reason why the sailor, attracted so much attention was that they refused to abandon their nautical habits. A naval brigade which landed to assist the loyalist cause during the Carlist Wars in Spain in 1837, actually constructed a fort that was shaped like a

Admiral Robert Fitzroy
This leading marine surveyor and meteorologist was best known for his famous survey of the coast of South America in HMS Beagle from 1831-34

Captain William Parry
Captain Parry was a great Arctic explorer and made four voyages in search of the North-west passage around North America

Captain Sir John Franklin
Perhaps the greatest Arctic
explorer of all, Sir John was
tragically killed when his
1845 expedition failed

Captain Francis McClintock
Captain McClintock was the man
who commanded the expedition
that found the last sad traces
of Franklin's expedition
in 1859

HMS Erebus and Terror
Franklin's ships in his last,
ill-fated expedition

**The Arctic council — the
council that never met!**
Many expeditions co-ordinated
from the Admiralty were sent
in search of Franklin although
the 'council' represented in
this multiple portrait never
actually met

**Crossing the Line
ceremonies in HMS Beagle**
This etching by the expedition's
artist, C Martens, shows how
little this ceremony has changed
in 150 years

The long arm of seapower

The Navy was also much involved in the many colonial campaigns of the period. Warships were usually first on the scene at trouble spots and often a crisis was resolved by the use of naval forces alone

ship. Brigadier Leeson, who was in overall command of the artillery during the Punjab campaign of 1848 and had under him a party of European sailors from the Indian Navy, noted with amusement that '...they looked upon their batteries as ships, their 18 pounders as so many sweethearts and the embrasures as portholes...' When a naval brigade from HMS *Shannon*, under Captain William Peel VC, helped to suppress the Indian Mutiny in 1857, General Colin Campbell noted that even their tactics seemed to be naval. The Brigade's heavy guns were used in the siege of a large mosque, the Shah Nujeef, and Campbell wrote later: 'Captain Peel behaved very much as if he had been laying the *Shannon* alongside an enemy frigate...' Nonetheless these tactics were successful and it was generally noted that the seamen's unorthodox methods seemed to work very well. Commander J W Gambier served with a naval brigade during the Second New Zealand War (1860-1866) and he recalled in his memoirs that:

'...our camp and ship life differed very little...we simply kept ordinary sea watch, with bluejackets on the lookout, accustomed to have their weather-eye open...a lieutenant walking about night and day...and half the men sitting about with their rifles ready to sping out when called with the same alacrity as if they had to shorten sail in a squall. Boatswain's Mates went about with their whistles..."bells" rang regularly every hour and half hour sea-fashion, lights went out and "rounds" took place with the ordinary routine to which we were all accustomed...'

As a result of this watchfulness — which, needless to say, he thought compared very favourably with the lamentable slackness

The Syrian campaign 1840 - amphibious operations
Britain helped Turkey in her war against Egypt. The Mediterranean fleet blockaded the coasts of Egypt and Syria and carried out raids on key coastal towns such as Tortosa, shown here

Japanese War — the Daimio of Satsuma and his entourage
Britain wished to trade with Japan but certain reactionary Daimios (Princes) such as Satsuma (centre) objected to Western infiltration. Their followers harassed European settlers and so British naval forces intervened

of the Army — the Commander was able to comment smugly: '…we never had an ugly rush and men tomahawked in our tents which, however, did happen to the soldiers…'

Observers who were used only to the Army found the sailors remarkably cheerful and willing. Indeed, Alexander Kinglake, who wrote an eight-volume account of the Crimean War, thought that the average sailor who served ashore in the naval brigade in the Crimea did not know his own strength!

'…He pulls strong carts to pieces as if they were toys. He piles up shot cases in the ammunition wagons till the horses fall under the weight, for he cannot understand "the ship starting till the hold is full"…'

But this strength enables him to march 72 miles in three days under a blistering Indian sun during the Mutiny or to man a rocket battery 400 miles inland during the Abyssinian campaign of 1867-8. A war correspondent who accompanied this particular expedition thought that the sailors '…were beyond dispute the "elite" of the force…' and went on to tell of their unusual behaviour:

'…Of an evening if we have a halt Jack Tar (of the Naval Rocket Battery) sometimes dances. The band of the Punjabi Pioneers - between whom and the sailors there is a great friendship although of course they do not understand a word of each other's language—comes over to the sailors' camp and plays dance music; and half a dozen couple of sailors stand up and execute quadrilles, waltzes and polkas…The sailors dance without the least idea that there is anything comic in the business; while around stand a crowd of amused soldiers and astonished natives of the country to whom the whole thing was a mystery…'

And Mrs Henry Duberly, the wife of an army officer who went out to the Crimea with her husband, in 1854, was most impressed by the men of the naval brigade who she encountered:

'…These seamen appear to work with the greatest energy and goodwill. One meets a gang of them harnessed to a gun and drawing with all their might and main; or digging at entrenchments singing, laughing and working heartily and cheerily…There was certainly no camp in which more kind consideration for others, more real active help, has been afforded to all than in that of the sailors; and their cheerfulness and willingness to labour encouraged and comforted all through the difficulties and sufferings of the last winter…'

Such attractive qualities, combined with his undoubted heroism, displayed time and again, did much to dispel the old, rather disreputable image of the sailor. To the Victorians, he was known simply as 'The handyman'.

Predictably enough, service ashore in the naval brigades was very popular with both officers and men. The work, although arduous and even dangerous at times, was a welcome relief from the monotony of ship routine and there was usually a little glory and occasionally some medals to be gained from it. Above all, a successful campaign was marked almost invariably by a spate of special promotions—a very welcome reward at a time when the Navy List was so long and the amount of active posts so small. But the brigades were not popular with the Admiralty, nor with the

more far-sighted officers who realised that the main business of a Navy was to be in constant readiness to fight at sea. In 1860, Lieutenant Albert Battiscombe, the first lieutenant of HMS *Pelorus*, whose crew had just returned to their ship after taking part in the opening stages of the Second New Zealand War, noted sadly in his private journal:

'...Am afraid the Commodore inteds to land again, if so, I cannot tell how the ship will be kept in order; even as it is, the men are not half the sailors they were before we landed and it will take at least two months seawork to get them at all ship shape...'

All the same, such opinions were very seldom expressed out loud and, however much the Admiralty might disapprove, the commanders on the spot were always ready to claim that they had landed only because the situation was so grave that any other decision would have been impossible! The great contribution made by the sailors ashore during the Crimean War and the Indian Mutiny established the brigades as an integral part of naval tradition — a tradition that is still recalled today in the famous field gun runs at the annual Royal Tournament in London.

The patience of the long anti-slavery patrols; the seamanship and endurance of the explorers and hydrographers; the panache of the river campaigns and the adaptability of the naval brigades — all these qualities were called into use when the Crimean War broke out on March 27 1854. And yet that war is chiefly remembered as a costly fiasco, in which the heroism and the sacrifice of ordinary British officers and men was shamefully

Japanese War — the Battle of Shimonoseki September 1864

The war was decided by the successful silencing of strong batteries defending the key Straits of Shimonoseki. (this *Illustrated London News* engraving of a captured Japanese battery was obviously copied from

wasted by the inefficiency and weakness of the High Command. The failings of the Army are well-known but the Navy, too, had its share of disappointments. At the outset of the war, the Mediterranean fleet was sent to the Black Sea where, having successfully escorted the French and British armies to the Crimea, the battleships remained impotent and inactive for the duration of the conflict. The Russians withdrew their fleet behind their powerful fortifications at Sebastopol and refused to venture out to do battle. As a result, the only major action was the Bombardment of Sebastopol on October 17 1854, which was notable simply because it was the first naval action in which all the battleships fought under steam power. Those which had engines used them, the rest were towed into action by small steamers that had been lashed to their unengaged side. A total of 44 British were killed and 266 wounded; three battleships were so badly damaged that they had to be sent to Malta for repairs and a vast quantity of shot and shell was expended. The massive Russian batteries, which had endured a concentrated fire from 25 French and British battleships, at ranges of between 1000 and 2000 yards, remained virtually unscathed, although 1100 Russians were killed or wounded.

Another hastily raised fleet was sent into the Baltic Sea under the immensely popular 'Charlie' Napier but, once again, the Russians refused to give battle and so the capital ships were left with very little to do. Napier was by then well past his prime and most accounts agree that he was overwhelmed by the great responsibility of his command. Like Admiral Jellicoe in 1916, he realised that he could easily lose the war in a day by allowing the powerful Russian fleet to slip past him into the North Sea or the Channel. Moreover, although his force was composed almost entirely of steamships — indeed, the first all-steam battlefleet of any size that Britain had ever assembled — it was, as we have already seen, extremely badly manned. As a result, Napier did not feel confident enough to take the offensive until August 1854, when he attacked and captured Bomarsund, an outlying Russian stronghold on the Aland islands in the middle of the Baltic — and even this operation was forced upon him by intense public pressure in England. In fairness to Napier, it must be said that his successor Rear-Admiral the Hon. Richard Dundas, who was 16 years his junior, behaved in an equally hesitant fashion when he took over the Baltic command in 1855, and his only major achievement was a spectacular bombardment of the Russian naval arsenal at Sveaborg. Much government property was destroyed but the fortifications remained unscathed and no attempt was made actually to capture the port. A contemporary song reflected the general disappointment in the Navy's performance:

'Two hundred and forty three vessels of war!
What did we build this big fleet for?
To go to the Black and the Baltic main
And what did it do? It came back again!'

However, this attitude was based upon an over-simplified view of seapower. A generation raised on stories of the Nile and Trafalgar, confidently expected that another Nelson would arise

River warfare

Naval forces were extensively used in countries such as Burma and China, where rivers were the only means of communication. Key towns could be attacked and fully equipped expeditions could be transported by small ships

to smash the Russians in yet another resounding naval victory. But there was no need to fight such a battle. By withdrawing their fleets into harbour at the outset of war, the Russians had conceded command of the seas to the French and British. The question facing the allied admirals was therefore not how to obtain command of the seas, but, rather, how that command was to be exercised. Unfortunately, such decisions were not left entirely to the admirals. A major novelty of the Crimean war was the important role played by the press, aided by the fact that the development of the electric telegraph enabled rumours and brief news items to travel much faster than the more detailed reports of the commanders in the field. Moreover, there was no censorship and, worst of all, the Admiralty and the War Office allowed themselves to be dictated to by popular opinion. The newspapers, led by J T Delane, editor of *The Times*, were naively bellicose, demanding spectacular victories of the Waterloo and Trafalgar type, and it was at their insistence that expensive showpieces such as the Bombardment of Sveaborg were undertaken. The newspapers did much useful work during the Crimean War, particularly in exposing the inefficient organisation of supplies and the appalling hospital conditions, but their influence on the strategic conduct of the war was excessive and harmful.

The Crimean War was undoubtedly a costly and even unnecessary mess but that is no reason why our opinion of its naval strategy should continue to be coloured by the naive judgments of the contemporary press. In fact, with the advantage

First Burma War 1824-26

British and Indian troops mount a river-borne attack on Burmese stockades on the Rangoon River. On the right is the Diana, the first steamer ever to go into action

First China War 1840-1842
HEICS Nemesis (right background), an early iron war steamer, sinks Chinese junks in Anson's Bay during her highly successful commission under Captain William Hutcheson Hall

of hindsight, it is possible to argue that seapower had enjoyed a limited success. In the Baltic, especially during the second campaign of 1855, Russian sea-borne trade was almost completely stopped by the close blockade of the smaller ships although coastal trade was able to continue spasmodically. Most important, the energetic younger commanders of the fleet carried out an incessant campaign of hit and run attacks on shore installations, which forced the Russians to maintain a large army in the north. In the Crimea, the small ships were used to even greater effect. In 1855, a well-organised expedition penetrated the Sea of Azoff, the north eastern arm of the Black Sea and, in a series of lightning raids, succeeded in halting all sea-borne supplies and reinforcements to Sebastopol, as well as bringing the war a little closer to the heartland of Russia. And, in October 1855, came the most efficient combined operation of the war. A British and French force — including the first ironclads or 'armoured batteries' — bombarded the powerful fortress of Kinburn which guarded the approaches to the important naval arsenal of Nikolaiev. The action lasted only a few hours and, in direct contrast to the gallant failure before Sebastopol exactly one year earlier, the ships managed to damage seriously the massive Russian fortifications — a success due in large part to the armoured batteries, which were able to pour in a concentrated fire from almost point blank range, without themselves suffering any serious damage. Sebastopol had already fallen and this direct threat to another of their important bases, coupled with the Baltic fleet's gradually increasing stranglehold on trade, encouraged

Second China War — the capture of Canton 1856
Sailors landing to form a Naval Brigade which took part in the assault on the key Chinese town of Canton

Second China War — the battle of Fatshan Creek 1857

This was a classic river action during which
British boats attacked and defeated a fleet of Chinese
junks. In the centre, Commodore Henry Keppel's
gig is sinking

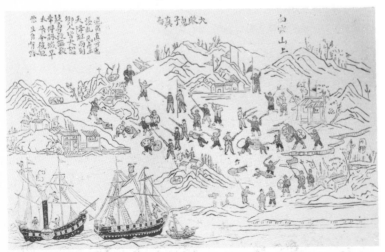

146

The Battle of Fatshan Creek
The Chinese view of the battle of Fatshan Creek

Army support
The adaptability of the sailor caught the public
imagination. He seemed to be able to perform any
task — from trench digging to rocket firing. The most
common nickname for a sailor was 'The handyman'

the Russians to make overtures for peace. The negotiations
dragged on until the spring of 1856 but eventually, on March 30,
the Treaty of Paris was signed.

In general terms therefore, it can be claimed that the Navy
emerges from the Crimean War with its laurels slightly less
tarnished than those of the Army. In heroism, there was nothing
to choose between the two services — the records of the Victoria
Cross show that soldiers and sailors alike were capable of the
highest acts of couage. As for actual achievements, the efficient
work of the small ships tends to tip the balance in the Navy's
favour. And in the field of supply and organisation — such an
important feature of this unhappy war — the Navy did much
better than its sister service. The internal running of the
individual ships and the system of supply for the fleets had
shown little of the inefficiency which so bedevilled the Army. The
care of the Navy's sick and wounded was immeasurably better
and it should also be acknowledged that there was far more
confidence and mutual respect between officers and men in the
Navy. Although the transitional fleet was in the throes of
adjusting to new technology and to different social conditions, it
had managed, nevertheless, to give a reasonably good account of
itself when the test of war came. That was an achievement which
augured well for the future, as the Navy returned from its war
stations to face up to the greatest change of all — the coming of
the ironclads.

Indian Mutiny 1857

Under the direction of Captain William Peel V C (right with sword raised), sailors from HMS Shannon haul up heavy guns during the relief of Lucknow

Second New Zealand War 1864

Sailors of the Naval Brigade lead the assault on the powerful Maori fortress Gate Pa. The attack was repulsed with heavy loss of life

Admiral of the Fleet Sir Henry Keppel

A distinguished and popular Victorian naval officer, Admiral Keppel made his name in China during the Second China War and later as C-in-C of the station

Abyssinian Campaign — the Naval Rocket Brigade

One hundred men were supplied by the Navy to form a special rocket brigade. They were commanded by Commander Fellowes — the officer on horseback

The Crimean War 1854-56

1. THE BALTIC CAMPAIGNS: Although the main war effort was directed in the Black Sea, the allies also sent fleets to the Baltic in 1854 and again in 1855. The Russians refused to give battle and so the capital ships had little to do. But the small ships successfully harassed Russian trade and carried out hit and run attacks

The allied Admirals

France and Britain allied themselves with Turkey to stop Russian expansion in the Balkans. It was an uneasy alliance and there was much friction between the various commanders

Preparing HMS Euryalus for war 1854

The war is chiefly remembered as a costly fiasco — but the Navy's systems of preparation and supply worked much better than that of the Army. Only recruitment proved a major problem

Napier leaving Portsmouth

Napier was tremendously popular and the public expected him to win instant, decisive victories. Huge crowds gathered to give him an enthusiastic send-off at Portsmouth

Admiral Sir Charles Napier

Napier (seen here as a Captain in about 1840) had a distinguished record and a reputation for dash and verve. In 1854, when he became C-in-C of the first Baltic campaign he had lost much of his old vigour

The Baltic Fleet running for Dover Straits
After being inspected by the Queen (see page 119),
Napier's fleet sailed for its war station. All the ships
were steamers, headed by the magnificent flagship HMS
Duke of Wellington (centre)

'Sharpen your cutlasses'
At the outbreak of war on April 4, 1854, Napier made
a long signal to the fleet which included the words 'Lads!
Sharpen your cutlasses and the day is your own!' This
rather out of date exhortation caused much amusement

Accident on board HMS Cruiser
The hazards of campaigning in
the the Baltic were many. At
the end of the season, ice and
snow were a severe danger
both to equipment
and personnel

HMS Hecla and Arrogant at Eckness 1854 (left)

It was the smaller ships of the fleet which saw the most action. Here, HMS Hecla (in the distance) and Arrogant carry out a hit and run attack on the Port of Eckness

The war on trade (below)

The first prize of the war is towed into Portsmouth Harbour on April 21, 1854

The war on trade (left)

The paddle sloop HMS Bulldog (centre) accompanied by the gunboat Starling (right) intercepts trading vessels

Captain Hall of HMS Hecla (right)

After his success at Eckness, Captain Hall (centre right) went to Stockholm where he was given a hero's welcome

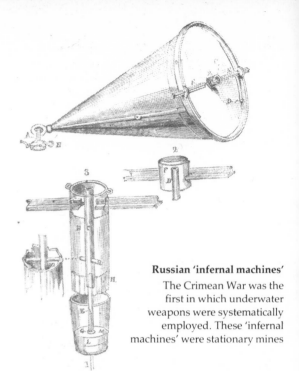

Russian 'infernal machines'

The Crimean War was the first in which underwater weapons were systematically employed. These 'infernal machines' were stationary mines

Explosion in HMS Exmouth

The destructive powers of the mines were little understood and they were often tinkered with by curious British officers, in this case with fatal results

HMS Merlin's escape

No British ship was lost by striking a mine, but the surveying vessel Merlin had a lucky escape while reconnoitring Sveaborg with the C-in-C Admiral Dundas on board

The Crimean War 1854-56

2. THE BLACK SEA CAMPAIGN: The main object of the Allies was to capture the important Russian naval arsenal of Sebastopol in the Crimea. Naval forces were unable to contribute much, although many sailors served ashore in the trenches. There were also some successful amphibious operations involving smaller ships in the Sea of Azoff and elsewhere in the Black Sea

Sebastopol from the sea

Viewed from the stern of HMS Sidon, an 8-gun paddle frigate. Her massive 56 pounder stern pivot gun is clearly shown

The bombardment of Sebastopol 1854

The first great assault on Sebastopol took place
on October 17. The naval bombardment was meant to
coincide with an all-out attack by the army but
the plans went awry and the ships found
themselves fighting alone

HMS Trafalgar and Retribution in action

This was the first major naval battle fought entirely
under steam. Those ships which had engines used them.
Sailing ships were towed into action by steamers
lashed to their unengaged side

HMS Albion towed to Malta for repairs
The powerful Russian forts remained virtually
unscathed but some of the ships were badly damaged
by shot and shell. HMS Albion lost eleven men
killed and seventy-one wounded. She was
sent to Malta for repairs

TIGER'S REVENGE

The bombardment of Odessa 1854

This was the first naval action of the Black Sea campaign. A small allied squadron bombarded the defences of Odessa and blew up the main magazine (shown here)

The capture of Yenikale 1855

The fortress of Yenikale which guarded the entrance of Azoff was abandoned by the enemy without a fight as the allies made their push into the sea in an attempt to cut the Russians' communications

FURTHER READING

Good books on the Victorian Navy are scarce but gradually, the subject is being studied in greater depth. Here are some of the best works available:

Technical

E Archibald	**The Wooden Fighting Ship 897-1860** (1968)
	The Metal Fighting Ship 1860-1970 (1971)
G A Ballard	**The Black Battlefleet** (1980)
J P Baxter	**The Introduction of the Ironclad Warship** (USA 1933)
O Parkes	**British Battleships 1860-1950** (1966)
A Preston & J Major	**Send A Gunboat** (1967)

Social

H Baynham	**Before the Mast** (1971)
D Jarrett	**British Naval Dress** (1960)
M Lewis	**The Navy in Transition** (1965)
	England's Sea Officers (1939)
G Penn	**Up Funnel, Down Screw** (1955)
E L Rasor	**Reform in the Royal Navy 1850-80** (1976)
G Taylor	**The Sea Chaplains** (1978)

Operations

C Lloyd	**The Navy and the Slave Trade** (1949)
Navy Records Society	**Russian War: Baltic & Black Sea 1854** (1943)
	Russian War: Baltic 1855 (1944)
	Russian War: Black Sea 1855 (1945)
	The Naval Brigades in the Indian Mutiny (1947)
	Second China War 1856-60 (1954)
G S Ritchie	**The Admiralty Chart** (1963)
J O C Ross	**The White Ensign in New Zealand** (Auckland 1967)
G L Verney	**The Devil's Wind** (1956)

General

W L Clowes	**The Royal Navy, A History Vols 6 & 7** (1897-1903)
P M Kennedy	**The Rise and Fall of British Naval Mastery** (1976)
J Winton	**Hurrah for the Life of a Sailor** (1977)